CAPITAL FORMATION AND EMPLOYMENT GENERATION IN RURAL INDIA

The Author

Dr. Mahi Pal (b. 1955) is currently working as Research Officer in the National Commission for SC&ST, Ministry of Welfare, Government of India. Recently, he had been on Post Doctoral Fellowship at the Institute of Social Sciences, New Delhi where he specialised in the field of Decentralised Planning and Panchayati Raj.

Dr. Mahi Pal has published several outstanding research papers in the areas of decentralised governance and rural development and is actively engaged in research. His previous publications include Land Productivity and Employment in Indian Agriculture; Ateet, Vartman Aur Bhavishya (in Hindi); and Critical Review of several state Panchayat Acts. He has also participated and contributed papers in various National and International Conferences/Seminars. The Author is also a member of several national associations in academic bodies.

Capital Formation and Employment Generation in Rural India

A Case Study of Saharanpur District (U.P.)

MAHI PAL

MITTAL PUBLICATIONS
NEW DELHI-110059 [INDIA]

Publication of this volume is financially supported by the Indian Council of Social Sciences Research (ICSSR), New Delhi. The responsibility of the facts stated and conclusions reached is entirely that of author and not of the Council.

First Edition 1999

ISBN 81-7099-712-7

Editorial Office:

H-13, Bali Nagar,
New Delhi - 110015

Phone: 5163610, 5431361

Showroom:

4594/9, Daryaganj,
New Delhi - 110002

Phone: 3250398

Published and printed by Naurang Rai for Mittal Publications,
A-110, Mohan Garden, New Delhi-110059, India.

Phones : 5648028, 5648773
Fax : 91-11-5648725 *Gram* : Mittalbux

Dedicated
to

my wife

AKSHAIM

ACKNOWLEDGEMENT

I am grateful to the Indian Council of Social Science Research, New Delhi, for providing financial assistance for this project.

I express my sincere gratitude to Dr. N.J. Kurian, Adviser (FR), Planning Commission, Dr.K.D. Gaur, Assistant Director, ICSSR and Dr. S.P. Singh, Lecturer, Government Degree College, Hamirpur, U.P., for their help, constructive criticisms and suggestions at various stages of this work. I also express gratitude to Dr. B.S. Nagi, Senior Research Fellow-cum-Senior System Manager, Council for Social Development for his help in analysing the data.

For illuminating discussions, my thanks are due to the Project Director, Project Economist and Assistant Engineer, DRDA, Saharanpur, BDOs and Panchayat Secretaries at block level and Pradhans and other knowledgeable persons at Gram Panchayat level. I am also grateful to the staff of DRDA, Zilla Panchayat, Blocks and Gram Panchayats for providing relevant data to us. I am also grateful to the research investigators for collecting the primary and secondary data from the field.

MAHI PAL

PREFACE

The main objectives of the Jawahar Rozgar Yojana (JRY) have been creation of community assets and generation of additional employment opportunities for the poor in rural sector of the Indian economy. However, there are few studies on these aspects of the scheme. This volume critically examines the impact of the JRY on capital formation, employment and income generation etc. with a view to bridging the gap.

The impact of the Yojana has been examined by adopting 'Before and After' evaluation design. The concept of opportunity cost has been used to assess the net benefits that have accrued to the beneficiaries. Besides, people's participation through Gram Panchayats and Gram Sabhas in implementation of the scheme has been examined in the study. Based on the findings, a suggestive framework for recasting and redesigning the scheme has been given in the book.

The book would be useful to researchers, policy-makers and, in particular to rural developers, voluntary organisations and all those engaged in promoting rural development through employment generation and infrastructural development. It will be of special benefit as supplementary reading to social sciences departments of universities, institutes of Rural Development and Training and similar other bodies.

MAHI PAL

GLOSSARY

Jawahar	:	First name of the first Prime Minister of India
Rozgar	:	Employment
Yojana	:	Scheme
Panchayati Raj	:	Rural local self-government
Awas	:	Housing
Gram	:	Village
Nyaya	:	Justice
Pacca	:	Cemented
Kachha	:	Earthen
Khadanjas	:	Vertical brick laying
Padanjas	:	Horizontal brick laying
Shramdan	:	Voluntary contribution
Zilla	:	District
Gram Vikas	:	Rural Development
Gram Sabha	:	Village Assembly
Pradhan	:	Chairperson of Gram Panchayat

ABBREVIATIONS

JRY	:	Jawahar Rozgar Yojana
NSS	:	National Sample Survey
IRDP	:	Integrated Rural Development Programme
TRYSEM	:	Training of Rural Youth for Self Employment
DWCRA	:	Development of Women and Children in Rural Areas
NREP	:	National Rural Employment Programme
RLEGP	:	Rural Landless Employment Guarantee Programme
EAS	:	Employment Assurance Scheme
DDP	:	Desert Development Programme
CADP	:	Command Area Development Programme
ITDP	:	Integrated Tribal Development Programme
MNP	:	Minimum Needs Programme
PRIs	:	Panchayati Raj Institutions
NGOs	:	Non-Governmental Organisations
JLNRY	:	Jawahar Lal Nehru Rozgar Yojana
DRDA	:	District Rural Development Agency
MWS	:	Million Wells Scheme
IAY	:	Indira Awas Yojana
MB Block	:	Muzaffara Bad Block

RM Block	:	Rampur Maniharan Block
SC	:	Scheduled Caste
ST	:	Scheduled Tribe
DSCO	:	District Soil Conservation Office
GP	:	Gram Panchayat
KP	:	Kshethra Panchayat
ZP	:	Zila Panchayat

CONTENTS

1

INTRODUCTION

Introduction

In this chapter a macro view of rural poverty and its alleviation strategies, genesis of Jawahar Rozgar Yojana (JRY), objectives of the study and research methodology are discussed:

Strategies of Rural Employment Generation

Poverty can be defined as deprivation of some segment of population in terms of income and consumption. This deprivation can be absolute and/or relative. The first means the poor are deprived of even the absolute minimum level of consumption. The second means the deprivation of the poorer sections in relation to the rich sections of the society. The main focus of the development planning in India since independence has been on eradication of absolute poverty. However, the reduction of the relative form of poverty has also been aimed at by providing access of the poor to growth opportunities and reducing the disparities in the distribution of resources.

To measure poverty, the planners have evolved the concept of poverty line which is measured in terms of minimum requirement for maintaining the physical well being of a person. The Task Force on Minimum Needs and Effective Consumption Demand, constituted by the Planning Commission (1979), determined the poverty line on the basis of per capita daily calorie requirement of 2400 in rural areas and 2100 in urban areas. Subsequently, at 1984 - 85 prices the poverty line for rural areas has been estimated at Rs. 6400 per annum per family. Recently, the poverty line has been reassessed by the Planning Commission as Rs. 11,060.00 on the basis of 1991-92 prices and the same has been used during the Eighth Plan period.

On the basis of this calories criterion the incidence of poverty and the ratio of the rural population living below the poverty line have been estimated from time to time by various experts and by the Planning Commission. These estimates have been based on the quinquennial surveys of consumption expenditure by the National Sample Survey (NSS). As per this survey, during 1987-88, about 33 per cent of the rural population was living below the poverty line. Khanna (1987) went one step ahead and categorized the poor families into four groups on the basis of the intensity of poverty as shown in the 38th round (1983-84) of the NSS data as follows :

Groups	*Income Range (in Rs)*	*No. of Household (in Million)*	*Percentage*
Destitues	Less Than 2265	0.99	2.20
Very Very Poor	2265-3500	6.13	13.80
Very Poor	3500-5000	16.93	38.20
Poor	5000-6400	20.25	45.80
Total		44.30	100.00

The poor are not a homogeneous group. There are considerable variations in the incidence of poverty among various sections of the poor. Status of employment, risk taking capacity, credit worthiness, entrepreneurship, socio-economic conditions and access to the anti-poverty programmes determine their poverty. The predominating section among the poor are the agricultural labourers and marginal farmers belonging to the Scheduled Castes (SCs) and Scheduled Tribe (STs). Prasad (1990) estimated that about 50 per cent of the SC households and 40 per cent of the ST households are of agricultural labour. Further, Bhattacharya (1988) estimated that these households have the lowest per capita consumption levels (Rs. 79.6 for the SCs and Rs. 79.9 for the STs) as against Rs. 120.2 of the others.

Just as the poor are not a homogenous group poverty too is not evenly distributed across the country. Its ratios range, as per the Planning Commission, from 7.20 in Punjab to 48.36

in Bihar. It is well recognized that both agricultural and industrial production have increased since independence as is evident from the gross domestic product which has registered about 4 per cent growth per annum. But the backward areas and poorer sections of the society have not been benefited by this growth. Instead, the gap between the rural and the urban areas has been widened. Regional disparities have also increased. To add insult to injury, the employment scenario has also worsened because the average rate of growth of the labour force (2.5 per cent) has been more than that of employment (2.2 per cent).

Removal of poverty in India has always been one of the main objectives of planning since its inception. But till the Third Five Year Plan, the emphasis had been on the growth in Gross National Product and it was assumed that it would trickle down to the masses and alleviate their poverty. But the fruits of growth did not trickle down to the masses as had been assumed. Even the green revolution had byepassed both the poor and the backward areas. So, during the Fourth Five Year Plan (1969-74), this approach to removing of poverty was modified. Special programmes were initiated to benefit the poor and the backward areas. As poverty is an indivisible, multidimensional phenomenon, for removing it a variety of programmes have been launched over a period of time. This strategy of poverty alleviation may be divided into five groups.

(i) Self-Employment Generation Programmes

These programmes offer self-employment to the poor by way of providing subsidized loan to purchase asset for augmenting their income. Integrated Rural Development Programme (IRDP), Training of Rural Youth for Self Employment (TRYSEM), Development of Women and Children in Rural Areas (DWCRA) are some of these self-employment generation programmes.

(ii) Wage-Employment Generation Programme

Under these wage employment is offered to the poor on various public works. Jawahar Rozgar Yojana (JRY) which came into being after merging the erstwhile National Rural Employment

Programme (NREP) and Rural Landless Employment Guarantee Programme (RLEGP), Employment Assurance Scheme (EAS) and MPs' Local Development Scheme come under this category of the programmes.

(iii) Special Area Development Programmes

These programmes are aimed at development of infrastructure in the backward areas which also give employment to the under-privileged. Drought Prone Area Programme (DPAP), Desert Development Programme (DDP), Hill Area Development Programme (HADP), Command Area Development Programme (CADP) and Integrated Tribal Development Programme (ITDP) come under this head.

(iv) Minimum Needs Programme (MNP)

These are programmes to develop infrastructural facilities in rural areas and to cater to the basic needs of the rural people. Elementary and Adult Education, Rural Health Rural Water Supply, Rural Roads, Rural Electrification, Rural Housing, Environment, Nutrition, Rural Domestic Cooking Energy, Rural Sanitation, Public Distribution System (PDS) come under this category of programme.

(v) Institutional Reforms

This stream of programmes, are aimed at reform and revitalisation of the grassroots institutions such as the Panchayati Raj Institutions (PRIs) to provide viable and effective platform for people's participation and decision making. Revitalisation of PRIs, land reforms and supporting the activities of Non-Governmental Organisation (NGOs) constitute such programmes.

Thus, a multipronged strategy has been adopted to alleviate poverty and acclerate rural development.

Genesis of the JRY

The Sixth Five year Plan was centred around the alleviation of poverty. The strategy aimed at redistribution of income and consumption in favour of the poorer sections of society by increasing employment opportunities in the rural area. To achieve this objective, the NREP was started in 1980.

Subsequently in 1983, the RLEGP was also launched to improve and expand the employment opportunities for the rural landless labourers with a view to providing guarantee of employment, for at least one member of all rural landless household for 100 days in a year. But the evaluation of the achievements of these programmes showed that even after 7 to 8 years of, their implementation more than 50 per cent of the villages did not have the benefit of any work programme at all. Besides, there was not much people's participation and involvement at the grass-roots level in selection of items of, the works and identification of the beneficiaries. To overcome these problems, a new scheme, Jawahar Lal Nehru Rozgar Yojana (JLNRY) was announced by the Union Finance Minister in his Budget Speech for the year 1989-90 with a provision of Rs.500 crores to implement it in 120 districts where the unemployment and poverty were acute. These funds were an additional allocation to the NREP and RLEGP to provide additional employment opportunities in the backward areas of the country. But with the view of making the rural employment programmes more effective and people oriented, the NREP, RLEGP and JLNRY on Ist April 1989 were merged into a single rural employment programme to be known as Jawahar Rozgar Yojana (JRY). The expenditure under the Yojana was shared between, the Centre and the States on 80:20 basis. As the scheme encompasses the whole of rural India, it is hoped, that it will create sufficient employment opportunities in the rural areas alongwith effective people's participation. The objectives of the scheme are twofold: primary objectives and secondary objectives. The Primary objective of the scheme is to generate additional gainful employment for the unemployed and under employed in the rural areas. The secondary objective is to create productive community assets for strengthening rural, economic and social infrastructures and to improve the overall quality of life in the rural areas.

Salient Features of the Yojana

(i) Share of the Centre and the States shall be 80:20.

(ii) Release of Central Share to districts directly.

(iii) Preference to SCs/STs for employment.

(iv) 30 per cent employment opportunities reserved for women.

(v) Special integrated project to meet the employment needs of the nomadic tribes.

(vi) DRDAs/Zilla Parishad and Gram Panchayats are responsible for implementation of the scheme.

(v) Pooling of resources of morc than one Gram Panchayat and Zilla Parishad is allowed.

(vi) Preferably, work under the scheme should be taken up during lean season.

(vii) Foodgrains shall also be given as a part of wages to the workers.

(viii) Contractors/Middleman are not allowed to have any hand in execution of the works.

(ix) Non-wage component not to be more than 50 per cent of the allocated fund.

(x) 5 per cent of the annual allocation is allowed to be spent on administrative or as contingent expenditure. A maximum of one fifth of the annual allocation can be spent on training of officials/non-officials involved in the implementation of JRY at the district and panchayat levels.

(xi) Resource allocation to the states/UTs under the scheme is made on the basis of incidence of poverty. From state to the districts the resources are earmarked on the basis of the per centage of agriculture labourers in the main workers in the rural areas, the per centage of the SC/STs population to the total rural population and inverse of agricultural productivity in the weight of 20:60:20 respectively.

Million Wells Scheme (MWS)

A scheme for construction of irrigation wells for SCs/STs called the Million Walls Scheme (MWS) was introduced during 1988-89 as a sub-scheme of NREP/RLEGP. This scheme is being continued under JRY.

Indira Awas Yojana (IAY)

IAY was an important sub-scheme of RLEGP aimed at construction of dwelling units for the poorest of the poor belonging to SCs/STs and freed bonded labourers. This scheme is also continued as a sub-scheme of JRY.

Statement of the Problem

As mentioned at the outset, a number of programmes have been launched since the beginning of planning after independence to alleviate poverty from rural India. Still the rural economy has been characterized by widespread unemployment, illiteracy and lack of access of a large section of the rural people to facilitate to meet their minimum needs which have resulted in widespread poverty in the villages. For instance, the percentage of population below the poverty line in the rural area during 1987-88 was about 33 which, although 18 per cent lower than that in 1977-78, is still high. Similarly, the situation as regards employment continues to be grim because during 1987-88 the rate of unemployment (usual status) in rural areas was 28 in case of males and 35 in that females as against 22 and 35 respectively ten years earlier. It means that the position has in fact worsened except for women over a period of time. The situation on the other fronts such as literacy and infrastructure in the rural areas is not an exception to this general decline.

One of the main reasons often mentioned for this situation is that although a target-oriented approach to alleviation of poverty has been adopted since the Fourth Plan, people have not been involved in the decision making process such as what work to undertake where and when to undertake it and for whom it should be taken up. As stated earlier, the evaluation studies of NREP and RLEGP had also revealed this drawback of the programmes. Therefore, in order to cover all villages and ensure people's participation and involvement all these programmes were merged and the JRY was launched. The objectives of this scheme, among others, are: generation of additional gainful employment for the unemployed and under-employed, creation and strengthening of rural economic infrastructure, creation of community social assets and assets in favour of rural poor for their direct and continuing benefit, positive impact on wage levels and overall improvement in the quality of rural life.

Thus, it is appropriate to examine the impact of this scheme on the socio-economic condition of the rural people in general and the rural poor in particular, and to assess as to what extent the objectives of the scheme have been translated into action by way of generating employment, particularly for the SCs/STs and the women, and creation of assets. What are the constraints in the fulfilment of the objectives of the scheme and what remedial measures should be taken to remove them. Whether an effective involvement and participation of the people under it has taken place. The Prime Minister had stated in Parliament on 28th April 1989 that "the Jawahar Rozgar Yojana is a programme aimed at placing in the hands of Village Panchayats around the country adequate funds to run their own rural employment schemes, in the interest of the vast masses of the rural poor who constitute the bulk of rural India. The Jawahar Rozgar Yojana aims at reaching every single Panchayat". Thus, the objectives with which the Yojana was launched need to be studied to find out to what extent the scheme has benefited those for whose it was designed.

Objectives, hypotheses and limitation of the study

Keeping in view the importance of the Yojana, the objectives of the study are as follows:

(i) To analyse the socio-economic characteristics of the beneficiaries,

(ii) To examine the impact of JRY on capital formation in rural areas,

(iii) To examine the impact of JRY on employment and income generation, and

(iv) To suggest measures for better implementation of the JRY

Hypotheses of the Study

The following hypotheses are proposed to be tested in this study:

(i) There is a positive relationship between employment generation, asset creation and income generation and the JRY Scheme.

(ii) Beneficiaries are not fully aware about the JRY in the sampled area.

Limitation of the Study

The following are the limitations of the present study.

(i) Workers do not maintain the records of their employment, income, and operational holdings. So, the responses of the workers about these aspects are mainly based on their memories

(ii) Although the scheme started during 1989-90 the relevant data regarding various aspects of the Yojana are not available which could have been drawn upon to fill the information gaps.

Research Methodology

Locale of the Study

The district of Saharanpur forms a part of the Meerut Division of Western Uttar Pradesh and is situated in its western corner. It is surrounded by Dehradun district on the North, Haridwar district on the East, Muzaffarnagar district on the South and Yamuna Nagar district of Haryana State on the west. Its geographical area is 3860 sq.kms which is about 1.3 per cent of that of Uttar Pradesh. This district has been purposely selected as it consists of both developed and under developed areas. Secondly, the author belongs to the rural area of this district and is therefore conversant with its socio-economic and cultural aspects. He will be able to collect correct information as he will not be treated as an outsider.

Sampling Design

A three - stage stratified random sampling design with Block as the first stage, Gram Panchayats at second stage and beneficiaries as the final or ultimate stage has been adopted for studying the impact of JRY on employment generation and capital formation. The stagewise selection procedure has been described below.

Selection of the Blocks

The district, which comprises of 11 Development Blocks, has been stratified into two areas, one under - developed and another developed, on the basis of the number of SCs/STs and agricultural labour, agricultural productivity, cropping intensity, per hectare application of chemical fertilizer, per centage of the net irrigated area to the net sown area, per capita production of foodgrains and the area under barren land. From these stratas so formed, one Block from each has been selected which is about 18 per cent of the total area of the district. The name of the underdeveloped Block is Muzaffara Bad (MB) and that of the developed Block is Rampur Maniharan (RM).

Selection of Gram Panchayats

Broadly, the JRY may be divided into three schemes viz General JRY, MWS and IAY. The selection procedure for GPs under these schemes has been given below:

(a) From each selected Block, a sample of 5 per cent of Gram Panchayats (GP) has been taken randomly. In this way, 6 GPs from the MB Block and 5 GPs from the RM Block have been taken for detailed study. From each selected GP, all JRY works viz construction of roads, construction of buildings, including Panchayat Ghar and schools, boring of wells and minor irrigation work etc have been taken for studying the capital formation and employment generation.

(b) Under MWS, in addition to providing of bore wells to SCs/STs, conservation of soil and water resources has also been undertaken. Construction of bunds, levelling of land, drainage and tree plantation etc have also formed its part. In other words, community productive assets have been created. For this, a sample of 5 GPs-4 from the MB Block and 1 from the RM has been taken to study the impact of these assets on gross output and employment. It may be mentioned here that in the R.M. Block, there was only one GP where conservation of soil and water resources had been undertaken, and the same has been taken up for study. This is the addition to the boring of wells.

(c) Like MWS, IAY is another sub-scheme of the JRY. For that also two clusters of the houses constructed under it from two GPs have been sampled.

Selection of the Beneficiaries

A sample of 382 persons who have benefited under the general JRY, MWS and IAY has been taken to examine the impact of these schemes on employment, income and quality of life of the villagers in general and the beneficiaries in particular.

Reference Period

The reference period for the study is three years from 1990-91 to 1992-93. Initially, we thought of the period from 1989-90 to 1991-92. But no data and other details of the Yojana were available for the year 1989-90 as it was introduced in the middle of this year. To overcome this problem, we have chosen 1990-91 to 1992-93 as the reference period for the study.

Methods of Analysis of Data

Simple statistical tools such as averages and per centages have been used for arriving at the results. Besides, to find out the impact of social classifications, mandays generated under JRY, and those generated outside the JRY, the land possessed,number of wage earners and skilled and unskilled workers and income of the beneficiaries, Multiple Regression Analysis has also been used.

Both primary data which have been collected from the universe through structural schedules and secondary data which have been collected from the published literature, District Rural Development Agency (DRDA) Block Development Office, and GPs have been used in arriving at the conclusions of the study.

2

A PROFILE OF THE ECONOMY OF DISTRICT SAHARANPUR

Introduction

The District of Saharanpur is situated between 29" to 30.24" north latitude and 77.70 to 88.12 East latitudes. Its geographical area is 3860.00 sq. km. of which 490.80 sq. km. is covered by forests. From geo-topographical point of view it may be divided into three parts viz, flood prone area, Khadar and Bangar. During 1989-90, the maximum and minimum temperature was recorded at 43.00C and 2.90C respectively. The district consists of 4 Tehsils and 11 Development Blocks. The number of inhabited villages, GPs and Nyaya Panchayats is 1265,940 and 113 respectively in the district. In this chapter, beside discussing the economic profile of the district comparison of this profile with the economy of the state as a whole has also been made to assess its position in the state's economy.

Demographic Profile

Table 2.1 depicts the demographic features of the district as well as of the state at two points of time. In 1981 the total population of the district was 18,21,000 which was 1.64 per cent of the state's population. After a decade in 1991, the ratio of the population of the district to that of the state was almost the same. As per the 1981 Census, the population of the SCs in the district was 22 per cent of its the total population as

Table 2.1 : Demographic Features

Census	*SAHARANPUR*						*UTTAR PRADESH*					
	Total Pop.	*SC (%)*	*ST (%)*	*Sex Ratio*	*Density Pop.*	*% of Urban*	*Total Pop.*	*SC (%)*	*ST (%)*	*Sex Ratio*	*Density Pop.*	*% of Urban*
1	2	3	4	5	6	7	8	9	10	11	12	13
1981	1821	22.00	0.00	832	478	21.2	110862	21.2	0.2	885	377	17.9
1991	2302	22.50	0.01	855	595	25.4	139031	21.0	0.2	881	472	19.9

Source : Compiled from the Districtwise Indicator of Development, U.P. State Planning Institute, Lucknow, 1991 and Census Hand Book 1991.

against 21.2 per cent in the state. After a decade, this percentage has increased marginally while in the state the reverse has been the case. The population of the STs in the district was nil in 1981 as against 0.2 per cent in the state. Over a decade, the STs have shown their presence in the district and their population was 0.01 per cent of the district's total population while in the state its percentage remained the same. The sex ratio in the district (832) in 1981 was lower than that of the state (885). But after a decade, it has improved to 885 while it has deteriorated in the state to 881. The density of population and the ratio of the urban population to total population are higher in the district than in the state as a whole. What is interesting is that the percentage of the urban population to the total population in the district has declined by about 6 per cent as against its increase by about 11 per cent in the state. This shows that the migration of the population from the rural to urban areas has shown a declining trend in the district. The density of population has increased by about 24 per cent in the district as against 11 per cent in the state. Thus, except in respect of the sex ratio, density of population and ratio of the urban population to the total population, the picture in the district representative of the state.

Occupational Structure

Table 2.2 shows the occupational structure of the population as shown in the 1981 and the 1991 Censuses for both the district and at the state level.

The percentage of workers to the total population in the district in 1981 was about 30 as against about 31 in the state. After a decade, in the district it remained almost the same as against about 32 per cent in the state. The percentage change over the period shows that the ratio of workers to the total population in the district has increased by about 1 per cent as against by about 5 per cent in the state. The percentage of main workers in the total population has decreased by about 2 per cent in both the district and the state. The percentage of the cultivators in the total main workers has decreased in the district by 5.58 as against a 9.77 per cent decline in the state. As the table reveals, the reduction in the ratio was rather sharp in the state. In contrast, the percentage

Table 2.2 : Occupational Structure

Census	*Percentage of workers to total population*	*Percentage of main workers to total population*	*Percentage of cultivators to total main workers*	*Percentage of marginal workers to total main workers*	*Percentage of agricultural labour to total main workers*	*Percentage of workers engage in household enterprises to total main workers*	*Percentage of other workers to total main workers*
1	2	3	4	5	6	7	8
Saharanpur							
1981	29.59	29.22	34.77	1.31	28.69	3.09	33.45
1991	29.85	28.72	32.83	3.93	30.86	3.18	33.13
Percentage change over 1981 census	0.88	–1.71	–5.58	199.24	7.56	2.91	–0.97
Uttar Pradesh							
1981	30.72	29.22	58.56	5.11	15.99	3.69	21.76
1991	32.27	29.74	52.84	8.51	19.23	4.38	23.55
Percentage Change over 1981	5.05	1.78	–9.77	66.54	20.26	21.41	8.23

Source : Compiled from Districtwise development indicator, U.P. States Planning Institute, Lucknow, 1991.

of the marginal workers to total main workers has increased by about 200 points in the district as against by about 67 points in the state over the decade. The percentage of agricultural labourers in the total main workers has also increased by about 8 percentage points in the district and about 20 per cent in the state. The percentage of the workers engaged in household enterprises in the total main workers has also gone up by about 3 points in the district as against 21.41 points in the state. Thus, in the state they have increased about 10 times more than in the district. Lastly, the percentage of the other workers in the total main workers over this period has decreased by about 1 percentage point in the district as against a 8.23 per cent increase in the state.

It may be concluded from the above discussion that in the district the percentage of the main workers in the total population has decreased. Similarly, the percentage of the cultivators in the main workers has gone down. On the other hand, the percentages of the marginal workers and the agricultural labour in total main workers have registered an increase over the period. It shows that the number of the marginal workers and the agricultural labourers has increased in the district, which is natural when the number of the cultivators has declined. Another conclusion that can be drawn from the table is that self-employment has been replaced by wage employment. The state-level data over this period of time also shows almost a similar development but here the number of agricultural labourers shows a sharper increase than at the district level. In other words, the cultivators have become marginal workers over a period of time in the district, while in the state, they have been absorbed in agriculture and household industries.

Education Structure

As regards the educational level of the district as well as that of the state three aspects viz. literacy rates, number of schools per a lakh of population in different categories and students-teachers ratios in basic, senior basic and higher secondary schools have been chosen as indicators of the profile at the two points of time.

The total literacy rate in the district has increased by about 42 per cent between and 1981 and 1991 as against an increase of 53 per cent in the state. Similarly, the male and female literacy rates in the district have increased by about 38 and 56 per cent respectively as against about 44 and 81 respectively in the state. It is clear from these indices that the literacy rates showed a more positive trend in the state than in the district. Thus the district does not represent the state in this field and has in fact lagged behind the state as a whole.

The change in the number of Junior Basic Schools, Senior Basic Schools and Higher Secondary Schools per a lakh of population over the decade presents a dismal picture both in the district and in the state as cols. 5, 6 and 7 of table 2.3 reveals. For example, the number of Junior Basic Schools has declined by about 6 per cent in the district as against by about 12 per cent in the state. In the case of senior Basic Schools the decrease is of about 11 per cent in the district as against about 8 per cent in the state. The severety of the problem in the case of higher secondary schools is about the same at both the district and the state levels as the reduction noticed is about 20 per cent in both the cases.

As regards technical institutions such as Industrial Training Institute (ITIs) the situation is comfortable in both the district and the state as the number of such units has increased at both the levels. But in the case of polytechnic the ratio has decreased by 25 per cent in the district as against a 40 per cent increase in the state.

The students-teacher ratio in Junior Basic Schools and Senior Basic Schools in the district has decreased by 15.15, and 6.90 percentage respectively as against an increased by 33.33, and 57.14 percentage respectively in the state. In the case of Higher Secondary Schools the ratio has increased both in the district (73.33 percentage) as well as in the state (63.33 percentage). But the rate of increase has been higher in the district than in the state.

A comparative picture of these three aspects of the education profile shows that the state as a whole is better placed than the district as its educational development indicators have shown a more positive trend than has been witnessed in the case of the district indicators.

Poverty Profile

The population below the poverty line in the district has been

Table 2.3: Level of Education and Related Indicators

Census	*Literacy Rates*			*Number of Schools per lakh population*					*Students teacher ratio in*		
	Total	*Male*	*Female*	*Junior Basic School*	*Senior Basic School*	*Higher Secondary School*	*ITI*	*Polytechnic*	*Junior Basic School*	*Senior Basic School*	*Higher Secondary School*
1	2	3	4	5	6	7	8	9	10	11	12
Saharanpur											
1981	29.56	39.13	18.06	56	9	5	0.08	0.04	33	29	30
1991	42.11	53.85	28.10	47	8	4	0.12	0.03	28	27	52
Percentage change over 1981 census	42.46	37.62	55.59	(–)6.07	(–)11.11	(–)20.00	50.00	(–)25.00	(–)15.15	(–)6.90	73.33
Uttar Pradesh											
1981	27.16	38.76	14.04	65	12	5	0.06	0.05	39	21	30
1991	41.60	55.73	25.31	57	11	4	0.12	0.07	52	33	49
Percentage change over 1981 census	53.17	43.78	80.27	(–)12.31	(–)8.33	(–)20.00	100.00	40.00	33.33	57.14	63.33

Source : Compiled from Districtwise Indicators of Development, U.P., State Planning Institute, Lucknow, 1991 and Statistical Dairy, State Planning Institute, 1992.

given in Table 2.4. The Table shows that of the total 260512 families in the district, 178953 are living below the poverty line as determined by the revised (Rs. 11000) income criterion. Thus, 68.70 per cent of the total population is below the poverty line. As Khanna has classified the poverty stricken household as destitutes, very very poor, very poor and poor on the basis of an income range of less than Rs. 2265 to Rs. 5000-6400 (See Chapter 1), in the same fashion, but using a different income range of less than Rs. 4000 to Rs. 8500- Rs. 11000 the 1993-94 Action Plan of the IRDP of the district has classified similar households in the district. This classification of the poverty stricken household is based on the villagewise survey conducted in 1992.

Table 2.4: No. of Families below Poverty line in District Saharanpur

Category	*Income Range*	*No. of Families*	*Percentage of Families*
Destitutes	Below Rs. 4000	13688	7.65
Very very poor	Rs. 4000-Rs. 6000	58204.	32.52
Very poor	Rs. 6000-Rs. 8500	52503	29.34
Poor	Rs. 8500-Rs. 11000	54558	30.49
Total families below poverty line		178953	100.00
Total no. of families		260512	
Percentage of family below poverty line		68.7%	

Source : Action Plan of IRDP, 1994-95, DRDA, Saharanpur.

If we look at the poverty profile categorywise we find that of the total families below the poverty line, 7.65 per cent are destitutes having an income of less than Rs. 4000. The percentage of very very poor families having an income of between Rs. 4000 - Rs. 6000 is 32.52 while 29.34 per cent families are very poor having an income of between Rs. 6000 - Rs. 8500 and the rest (i.e. 30.40 per cent) are poor with an income of between Rs. 8520 - Rs. 11000. Here, it may be mentioned that comparable data for the state as a whole is not available and hence a comparative study has not been possible.

Agriculture

Table 2.5 presents the numbers and areas of the operational

Table 2.5: Size and Pattern of Operational Holdings

	Saharanpur						Uttar Pradesh					
	1980-81			1985-86			1980-81			1985-86		
Distribution of operational holdings	*No. of holdings (%)*	*Area of holdings (%)*	*Average size of holdings (ha)*	*No. of holdings (%)*	*Area of holdings (%)*	*Average size of holdings (ha)*	*No. of holdings (%)*	*Area of holdings (ha)*	*Average size of holdings (%)*	*No. of holdings (%)*	*Area of holdings (%)*	*Average size of holdings (ha)*
1	2	3	4	5	6	7	8	9	10	11	12	13
Less than 1ha	56.50	14.70	0.39	59.50	17.5	0.40	70.60	25.70	0.37	72.60	28.30	0.36
1-2ha	19.20	17.80	1.40	19.10	20.0	1.43	16.30	22.60	1.40	15.60	23.30	1.39
2-3ha	9.40	15.20	2.45	9.00	16.60	2.51	6.20	14.70	2.41	5.70	14.80	2.41
3ha & above	14.90	52.30	5.31	12.04	45.90	5.05	7.00	37.00	5.32	6.10	33.60	5.13

Source : Districtwise Indicator of Development, State Planning Institute, U.P., 1991.

holdings at two points of time viz. 1980-81 and 1985-86. The available categories of the holdings are : less than 1 hectare (ha), 1-2 ha, 2-3 ha and 3 ha and above. Let us take them one by one.

During 1980-81, in Saharanpur district, of the total number of operational holdings (OH) 56.60 per cent were of less than 1 hectare (ha), operating, 14.70 per cent of the total operated area, 19.20 per cent were of 1-2 ha operating 17.80 per cent of the total operated area, 9.40 per cent were of 2-3 ha operating 15.20 per cent of the total operational area and 14.90 were of 3 ha and above operating 52.30 per cent of the total operated area. An analysis of the numbers and areas of OHs reveals that those of less than 1 ha, which accounted for 56.50 per cent of the total OHs, operate only 14.70 per cent of the total operated area. In contrast, OHs of 3 hac and above which accounted for 14.90 of the total OHs operate as much as 52.30 per cent and the total operated area. If we compare this pattern with that of the state as a whole we find that it deviates from the latter as at the state level OHs of less than 1 ha which are 70.60 per cent of the total OHs, operate 25.70 of the total operated area and those of 3 ha and above which are 7.00 per cent of the total OHs operate 37.00 per cent of total operated area.

The average sizes of OHs of less than 1 ha, 1-2 ha, 2-3 ha and 3 and above ha in the district have been 0.39 ha, 1.40 ha, 2.45 ha and 5.31 ha, respectively. This pattern of average sizes of OHs of the district is more or less the same as the pattern at the state level.

During 1985-86, in the district of Saharanpur, of the total numbers of OHs, 59.50 per cent were of less than 1 ha operating 17.50 of the total operated area, 19.10 per cent were of 1-2 ha operating 20.00 per cent of the total operated area, 9.00 per cent were of 2.3 ha operating 16.60 of the total operated area and those of 3 ha and above accounting for 12.04 of the total OHs were operating 45.90 per cent of the total operated area. After comparing the numbers and areas of the OHs at the two points of time (1980-81 and 1985-86) we find that in 1985-86 the number of OHs of less than 1 ha and the area operated under them have been increased and the numbers and areas of OHs operated under the rest of the categories have decreased. This shows the impact of land reforms, particularly distribution of surplus land among the landless. At the state level also, the number and area of OHs operated under the OHs of less than 1 ha have increased and the number and area operated under the OHs of 3 ha and above have decreased over the period.

If we compare the average sizes of OHs in the district in 1980-81 and 1985-86 we find that the average size of OHs less than 1 ha 1-2 ha and 2-3 ha have increased although very little.

The situation that has emerged at the state level in this regard is however different level. Here, the average sizes of OHs of less than 1 ha and 1-2 ha have decreased over a period of time although the decrease is very little. The average size of OHs of 2-3 ha has remained as it was while that of OHs of 3 ha and above has also decreased. But there is no decrease in the average size of OHs of the rest of the categories. This shows that in the state as a whole land reforms have not made any categories. This shows that in the state as a whole land reforms have not made any impact on the re-distribution land in favour of the landless.

Table 2.6 gives the agricultural development indicators, both at the district and the state level, at two points of time. Eleven indicators have been selected to measure the level of agricultural development at the two levels. The percentage of the net sown area to the total agricultural land is higher for the district than for the state. The increase in this regard between 1980-81 and 1989-90, the two points chosen for a comparative study has also been higher in the district than in the state as a whole. ?The percentage of net irrigated area to net sown area is also higher in the district than in the state but the change noticed in this field over a period of time has been more in the state than in the district. Similarly, the percentage of gross irrigated area to gross sown area is higher in the district than in the state and the growth over a period of time also shows the same trend. The percentage of area under commercial crops is more in the district than at the state level but the growth over a period of time has been almost at the same pace which shows that the district as well as the state have been showing increasing preference for commercial crops at the cost of the food grain crops. Although the cropping intensity in the district is higher than in the

Table 2.6: Indicators of Agricultural Development

S. No.	Indicators	Saharanpur			Uttar Pradesh		
		1980-81	*1989-90*	*Percentage change over 1980-81*	*1980-81*	*1989-90*	*Percentage change over 1980-81*
1	2	3	4	5	6	7	8
1.	Percentage of net area sown to total Agricultural land	93.77	94.86	1.16	82.42	82.46	0.05
2.	Percentage of net irrigated area to net sown area	67.70	70.00	3.40	54.90	60.00	9.29
3.	Percentage of gross irrigated area to gross sown area	60.70	76.20	25.54	46.30	56.70	22.46
4.	Percentage of area under commercial crops to gross sown area	40.93	47.53	16.13	16.70	19.25	15.27
5.	Cropping Intensity	157.74	159.95	1.40	142.69	147.09	3.08
6.	Per ha consumption of fertilizer (kgs)	69.12	118.13	70.91	46.82	82.53	76.27
7.	Percapita food grain production (kg)	210.81	223.45	6.00	227.47	254.93	12.07
8.	Percapita production of pulses (kg)	4.41	4.38	–0.68	23.04	18.20	–21.01
9.	Per gross ha value of Agriculture production (at 1980-81) (Rs.)	6311.00	9898.00	56.84	4169.00	6118.00	46.75
10.	Per ha output of						
(i)	Wheat (qtls)	17.35	25.42	46.51	16.50	20.47	24.06
(ii)	Rice (qtls)	17.04	19.35	13.56	10.53	17.47	65.91
(iii)	Potato (qtls)	164.20	211.81	29.00	156.66	182.02	16.19
(iv)	Oilseeds (qtls)	8.13	11.24	38.25	5.27	7.40	26.64
(v)	Sugar cane (qtls)	525.28	591.28	12.56	470.90	553.12	17.46
11.	Per tractor available gross sown area (ha)	138.20	42.40	–69.32	262.10	105.90	–59.60

Source : Districtwise Indicator of Development, State Planning Institute, U.P., 1991.

state as a whole the increase registered at the state level over a period of time has been higher than in the district. The lower increase in the cropping intensity in the district could be a result of its having reached the saturation point. The per hectare consumption of fertilizer, however, when up by about 70 per cent. The per capita production of food grains in the district is less than that in the state and also the growth over a period of time has been less than in the state as a whole. The per capita production of pulses has declined at both the levels, but the decline has been comparatively sharper in the state.

The per hectare outputs of wheat, rice, potato, oilseeds and sugarcane show that the district has had an edge over the state in this area and the growth registered over a period of time has also been higher more in the district than in the state. This clearly shows that on the agricultural front, the district is more developed than the state.

In the district the per tractor available gross sown area was 138.20 ha in 1980-81 which fell to 42.40 in 1989-90 which means about 70 per cent reduction. For the state as a whole the per tractor available gross sown area in 1980-81 was 262.10 hectare which declined to 105.90 in 1989-90, that is by about 60 per cent. This indicator points to two trends. First, due to its demonstration effect, every farmer wants to have a tractor irrespective of the area of this land he possessed. Friendly Bank loaning for this purpose also induces them to have their own tractors. However, the fact that this per tractor area has come down shows that it has been proving unviable. Secondly, the reflection of this unviability in reduction of per tractor available area has been shaper in the district in comparison to the state.

An overall assessment of the state of agriculture in this district and the state clearly shows that the agricultural economy of the district is more developed than that of the state as a whole.

Industry

Table 2.7 presents the indicators of industrial development at both the district and the state level at two points of time, 1980-81 and 1987-88.

In this field also the district has put up a better performance than has the state as a whole. But the extent of change over a period of time has been in the state than it has been in the district as the different indicators of industrial development testify. The only exception is the number of large industrial units per a lakh of population where the percentage increase in the district is 125 as against only 16.67 in the state. The per labour value added for the district in 1980-81 was about Rs. 18000.00 (at current prices) which rose to about Rs. 66000.00 in 1987-88 whereas for the state as a whole, corresponding figures were Rs. 11000.00 and Rs. 49000.00 respectively. Thus, while the rate of increase for the district is 264.27 per cent it is 329.73 per cent for the state. The number of persons employed in registered units per lakh population was also higher in the district at both the points of time than that in the state. The same was the case with the per capita gross value of output and the number of working factories per lakh population but the change over the period has been more noteworthy in the state than in the district.

Socio-Economic Infrastructure

Table 2.8 depicts the socio-economic infrastructural development at both the district and state levels at two points of time (1980-81 and 1990-91). The Table also shows the degree of change over the period at both levels. The number of scheduled Banks per lakh population in the district was 4.8 in 1980-81 and 5.8 in 1990-91. It recorded about 21 per cent growth over this period. The corresponding numbers for the state were 3.7 and 6.3 respectively testifying to a growth of about 70 per cent between the two years. The number of cooperative marketing societies per lakh population was also higher in the district than in the state at the two points of time. But the number declined over the period and the rate of decline was almost the same at both the levels. It could will be the number of the cooperative marketing societies has remained the same during the period the population has increased. The number of Agricultural Credit Societies per lakh rural population in the district increased by 7.98 per cent over this period whereas in the state, their number decreased by 19.21 per cent. The number of Land Development Banks per lakh population has decreased by more than 13 per cent at both levels during the period.

Table 2.7: Indicators of Industrial Development

S. No.	Indicators	Saharanpur			Uttar Pradesh		
		1980-81	*1990-91 / 1987-88*	*Percentage change over 1980-81*	*1980-81*	*1990-91 / 1987-88*	*Percentage change over 1980-81*
1	2	3	4	5	6	7	8
1.	No. of large industrial unit per lakh population	0.04	0.09	125.00	0.06	0.07*	16.67
2.	Per labour value added [(Rs. '000) at current prices]	18.36	66.88	264.27	11.57	49.72	329.73
3.	Person employed in registered with per lakh population	1516.00	1107.00	(–)26.98	697.00	568.00	(–)18.51
4.	Per capita gross value of output (Rs.)	1142.95	2011.87	76.02	338.20	1091.04	222.60
5.	No. of working factories per lakh population	10.80	12.60	16.67	5.10	6.30	23.53

Source : Districtwise Indicator of Development, State Planning Institute, U.P., 1991.

Table 2.8: Indicators of Socio-Economic Infrastructural Development

S. No.	Indicators	Saharanpur			Uttar Pradesh		
		1980-81	1990-91	Percentage change over 1980-81	1980-81	1990-91	Percentage change over 1980-81
1	2	3	4	5	6	7	8
1.	No. of Scheduled Banks per lakh Population	4.80	5.80	20.83	3.70	6.30	70.27
2.	No. of cooperative marketing societies per lakh population	0.27	0.22	(–)18.52	0.23	0.19	(–)17.39
3.	No. of Ag. credit societies per lakh rural population	8.15	8.80	7.98	9.58	7.74	(–)19.21
4.	No. of LDB per lakh population	0.30	0.26	(–)13.13	0.23	0.20	(–)13.04
5.	Length of PWD pacca road per lakh population (kms)	34.95	48.27	38.11	43.58	53.04	21.71
6.	Length of PWD pacca road per 000 square kms area (kms)	165.09	284.71	72.46	162.34	243.78	50.17
7.	Per capita consumption of electricity (Kilowatt/hour)	138.40	169.60	22.54	83.60	159.90	91.29
8.	Consumption of electricity in Agri. as percentage of total consumption	25.4	41.00	61.42	30.20	34.30	13.58
9.	No. of electrified village (%)	53.73	95.71	78.13	37.64	73.35	94.87
10.	No. of post office per lakh population	11.00	9.40	(–)14.55	15.70	14.20	(–)9.55
11.	No. of telephone connection per lakh population	188.00	291.00	54.79	127.00	218.00	71.65

Source : Compiled from the Districtwise Indicator of Development, U.P. State Planning Institute, Lucknow 1991 and Census Hand Book 1991.

The length of PWD Pacca Roads per lakh population is higher in the state as a whole than in the district, but the increase in it over this period of time has been more in the latter than in the former. However, in the case of the length of PWD Pacca roads per thousand square kms area the figure for the district is higher than for the state and the growth rate over the period is also more for the district.

The per capita consumption of electricity is also higher in the district than in the state. But if growth rate is more in the state than in the district as the table shows. The consumption of electricity in agriculture as a percentage of total consumption is also higher in the district than in the state as a whole and the growth also has shown a similar trend. The percentage of electrified villages in the district in 1990-91 was about 96 per cent as against about 73 per cent in the state. It means that in this aspect also the district is better placed than the state. But if we look at the growth in rural electrification we fund that the state has had an edge over the district. The number of Post Offices per lakh population is also higher in the state than in the district. But their growth in both cases during the decade has been negative. A possible explanation for this decline could be a higher increase in the population than in that of the post offices. The number of telephone connections per lakh population is also more in the district than in the state. But here the growth over the period has been more in the state than in the district as the table shows. Thus, it may be concluded that from the point of view of socio-economic infrastructure the district is more developed than the state as a whole. But the rate of growth of the infrastructural facilities has been higher in the state than in the district.

Summing Up

This discussion may be concluded with the finding that the sampled district as a whole is more developed than the state. Among other factors, fertility of the land, its geo-topographical features and induction of green revolution in the early sixties have played important role in its development.

3

PROGRESS OF JRY IN THE DISTRICT

Introduction

In this chapter earmarking of funds for JRY for different scheme under it, utilisation of these funds, main assets created through it and the employment generated by it are discussed.

Earmarking of Resources

The earmarking of funds for JRY from DRDA and other agencies is as follows:

Of the total resources allocated to the district under JRY, 6 per cent is earmarked for IAY, 20 per cent for MWS and of the rest 20 per cent is retained by the DRDA. The remaining amount is divided between the Panchayats and the DRDA in 80:20 ratio. During the financial year (1993-94), the share of IAY and MWS have been raised to 10 per cent and 30 per cent respectively. Rs.50,000 has been retained by the DRDA for the training of the officials and non-officials. The rest has been shared by the Panchayats and the DRDA in 80:20 ratio.

The mechanics of implementation and execution of the different streams of JRY is like this. IAY and houses for the weaker sections have been implemented by the Chief Development Officer. The MWS scheme has been implemented by the different departmental agencies at the district level.

They are:

(a) Soil Conservation Office

(b) Soil Conservation Office, Ram Ganga Command I

(c) Soil Conservation Office, Ram Ganga Command II

(d) Irrigation Construction Division

(e) Rural Engineering Services

(f) Minor Irrigation from 1992-93 onward only for bore well.

The rest of the scheme, which is also called General JRY, has been implemented and executed by the GPs.

It may be mentioned here that the common notion that the JRY is implemented by the GPs is not true. As is evident from above only a part of the scheme is implemented by the Panchayats. The schemes such as IAY, MWS and construction of houses for the weaker sections have been implemented by the State Government Department stationed at the district headquarter.

Financial Allocation and Utilisation

The allocation of finance and its utilisation under JRY in the district during a three year period (1990-91 to 1992-93) are given in table 3.1. The annual outlay for the three years 90-91, 91-92 and 1992-93 - was Rs. 665.97, Rs 715.03 and Rs 891.28 lakhs respectively. This shows that the outlay had been stepped up year after year. During 1991-92, allocation under the scheme was about 7 per cent more than its level in 1990-91 and it was about 24 per cent higher in 1992-93 than in 1991-92. In contrast the balance from the previous year has been showing a negative trend as table 3.1 shows.

Table 3.1: Financial Allocation and Achievements

(Rs. in Lakhs)

S.No.	*Particulars*	*90-91*	*91-92*	*92-93*
1.	Annual Outlay	665.97	715.03	891.28
2.	Amount release by Govt.	665.97	715.03	891.28
3.	Balance of porevious year	146.04	96.50	55.82
4.	Total receipts	812.01	811.53	947.10
5.	Amount Unutilized on wage	446.20	446.95	535.75
6.	Amount Unutilized on non-wage	269.31	308.76	410.81
7.	Total Expenditure	715.51	755.71	946.56
8.	Ratio of Utilized fund to total receipt of fund	88.12	93.12	99.99

Source : Compiled from the office of DRDA Saharanpur, U.P.

During 1990-91 it was Rs. 146.04 but came down to Rs. 96.50 lakh in 1991-92 and further to Rs 55.82 lakhs in the folowing year. This is a healthy trend as the ratio of the unspent resources to the total allocation is declining. Including this unspent money, the total amount released for the district during 90-91,1991-92 and 1992-93 added up to Rs. 812.01, Rs.811.53 and Rs. 947.10 lakhs respectively. The total expenditure incurred during the three years was Rs. 715.51, Rs. 755.71 and Rs. 946.56 lakhs respectively. If we compare the total receipts to the total expenditure, we find that a gap of unspent resources. The ratio of the utilized funds to the total receipts worked out to 88.12, 93.12 and 99.99 per cent during 1990-91, 1991-92 and 1992-93 respectively. The ratio of the wage and non-wage expenditure has also been worked out for the three years. It varies from year to year. In 1990-91 it was 62:38 and came down to 59:41 in 1991-92 and further to 57:43 in 1992-93. This trend shows that the wage component of the expenditure has been declining sharply from year to year.

Creation of assets under the JRY

The main assets created during the reference period in the sampled district are given in table 3.2. The rural roads which include kachha roads, khadanjas (vertical brick laying), padanjas (horizontal brick laying) tanks/wells, field channels, land development, including levelling, soil and water conservation, culverts, new school and panchayat buildings or additions to the existing buildings, houses for SC/STs and the weaker sections and social forestry. Besides, the assets in the term of the houses for SC/ST constructed under IAY and conservation and preservation of soil and water resources under MWS have also been created in the district. The repairing of khadanjas is another important activity undertaken by the panchayats in the district.

As can be seen from table 3.2 the maximum expenditure has been incurred on construction of rural roads, particularly village streets. It accounts for more than one quarter of the expenditure incurred during 1990-91. These asset creation activities accounted for about 30 per cent of the total persondays generated during the year.

During 1991-92, these activities accounted for about 60

Table 3.2 : Main Assets created through Jry in Saharanpur District

Sl. No.	Sector	1990-91		1991-92		1992-93	
		Total expenditure incurred (lakhs)	*Total person-days generated (lakhs)*	*Total expenditure incurred (lakhs)*	*Total person-days generated (lakhs)*	*Total expenditure incurred (lakhs)*	*Total person-days generated (lakhs)*
1.	Rural Roads	191.99	6.74	438.54	12.67	235.24	11.79
2.	Tank/Well	1.01	0.05	—	—	—	—
3.	Field Channels	7.92	0.13	23.64	0.73	—	—
4.	Land Development	1.50	0.03	81.89	4.08	2.22	0.05
5.	Soil Conservation	0.20	0.01	77.37	1.88	—	—
6.	Culvert	4.28	0.09	—	—	9.55	0.08
7.	School Wall/Panchayat	1.01	0.01	3.53	0.02	5.97	0.14
8.	Khadanja Repairs	23.80	0.82	20.81	0.22	371.24	2.39
9.	SC/ST House	49.41	1.56	10.50	0.16	57.08	1.60
10.	Indira Awas Yojana	5.04	—	40.20	0.78	54.93	1.11
11.	Million Well Scheme (Land levelling)	16.20	0.73	—	—	193.63	6.23
12.	Social Forestry	—	—	0.90	0.04	5.0	1.50

Source : Compiled from the record of the DRDA, Saharanpur.

per cent of the total expenditure incurred during the year. As regards employment opportunities created during the year, it accounted for about 57 per cent of the total persondays generated.

But during 1992-93, their share in the total expenditure was about 25 per cent, much less than in the previous year. The persondays generated under these activities during the year accounted about 45 per cent of the total.

The reason for decline in the allocation under this head is that the requirement is being fulfilled.

Besides houses for the SC/STs culverts, and Khadanja repairs also accounted for a substantial share of the total expenditure incurred during the period.

Employment Generation

The table 3.3 depicts the class-wise and yearwise pattern of

Table 3.3 : Year/Classwise persondays generated under Jry

S.No.	*Year*	*1990-91*	*1991-92*	*1992-93*
1.	Total Mandays generated (lakh)	22.31 (100.00)	22.18 (100.00)	26.15 (100.00)
2.	SC	12.90 (57.82)	16.11 (72.63)	18.29 (69.64)
3.	ST	—	—	—
4.	Others	9.41 (42.18)	6.07 (27.37)	7.86 (30.06)
5.	Land Less	20.51 (91.93)	14.73 (66.41)	21.07 (80.57)
6.	Women	0.12 (0.54)	0.07 (0.32)	— —

Figures in Parenthesis are percentage of total.
Source : Compiled from the office of the DRDA, Saharanpur, U.P.

employment generation under the JRY during the reference period. The total persondays generated during 1990 -91, 1991-92 and 1992-93 were 22.31, 22.18, and 26.15 lakhs respectively. The employment generation during the first two years was almost the same while during 1992-93 it was about 17 per cent more than in these years. The reason for this increase is that in this year the persondays generated through schemes of other departments which got funds from the JRY were also included.

During 1990-91, of the total persondays generated, about 58 per cent were generated for the SCs and the rest for the others. As there is no ST population in the district, no employment was generated for them. But it may be mentioned that as per the 1991 census about 0.1 per cent of the total population was that of the STs who did not figure at all in the 1981 census. The total persondays generated, nearby 92 per cent were for landless and a mere 0.54 that is not even 1 per cent were for women. It may be noted that as per the guidelines for the JRY 30 per cent of the employment opportunities under the Yojana should be reserved for women. This shows the negligible participation of the women in the JRY scheme.

During 1991-92 of the total persondays generated, about 73 per cent were created for the SCs and the rest for the others. The share of the landless was about 66 per cent while other of the women was only 0.32 per cent.

During 1992-93, the share of the SCs in the total persondays generated was about 70 per cent whereas the share of the others was about 30 per cent. The share of the landless was about 81 per cent while that of the women was nil. If we see the trend of employment generation for the different categories we find the share of the SCs has been higher than that of the other category during the reference period. It was the highest in 1991-92 and for others it was the highest in 1990-91. The share of the landless was the highest during 1990-91 and the lowest during 1991-92. Women's share was negligible during the first two years which too vanished during 1992-93.

Summing Up

It may be said that the allocations under JRY to the district has been showing an increasing trend from 1990-91 onward. The same was the case with the utilisation ratio. The wage and non wage ratios have been almost as provided for in the guidelines.

Among the assets created under JRY rural roads generated the maximum employment in the rural areas ranging from 57.82 per cent to 72.63 per cent. Of the total persondays generated, 57.82 per cent, 72.63 per cent and 69.94 per cent have been created for SCs during the three years 1990-91, 1991-92 and 1992-93 respectively. The rest were generated for the other categories of workers. A very negligible share of the employment generation accrued to the women during the first two years with the third year giving a negative figure.

4

SOCIO-ECONOMIC PROFILE OF THE SAMPLED PANCHAYATS

Introduction

In this chapter, socio-economic profile of the pradhans, social composition of the population of panchayats, population below the poverty line and details of village officials are discussed.

Socio-economic Profile of the Pradhans

Table 4.1 shows the socio-economic profile of the Pradhans (chairpersons of the GP). All the pradhans in both the sampled Blocks were males. In MB Block, of the total 6 Pradhans, 2 were barely literate, 2 had passed the middle class examination one was a metriculate and one was graduate. In the other Block, of the total 5 Pradhans, 1 was illiterate, one had passed the middle class examination, one was a metriculate and one graduate. The village whose Pradhan was illiterate was Ghatra. Actually, this Pradhan was originally the Upa-Pradhan. When the Pradhan of this GP got elected as the Pramukh of the Kshetra Samiti, the Upa-pradhan became the Pradhan. The Pradhan of this GP who got elected as the Pramukh, was later nominated as the chairperson of the zilla parishad (ZP) of the district because of his being a leader of the ruling Samajwadi Party.

None of the Pradhans belonged to the SCs. They belonged to the other communities. All the Pradhans' in the MB Block

Table 4.5 : Socio-economic background of the Pradhans

S. No.	Particulars	M.B. Block		R.M. Block	
		No.	Percentage	No.	Percentage
1	2	3	4	5	6
1.	No. of Sampled Pradhans	6	100.00	5	100.00
	(b) Female			—	—
	(a) Male	6	100.00	5	100.00
	(b) Female	—	—	—	—
2.	Level of Education				
	(i) Illiterate	—	—	1	20.00
	(ii) Literate	2	33.33	1	20.00
	(iii) Primary	—	—	—	—
	(iv) Middle	2	33.33	1	20.00
	(v) High School	1	16.67	1	20.00
	(vi) Intermediate	—	—	—	—
	(vii) Graduate & above	1	16.67	1	20.00
3.	Social Group				
	(i) SC	—	—	—	—
	(ii) Others	6	100.00	5	100.00
4.	Occupation				
	(i) Agriculture	6	100.00	4	80.00
	(ii) Non-agriculture	—	—	1	20.00
	(iii) Service	—	—	—	—
	(iv) Others	—	—	—	—
5.	Land Possessed				
	(i) Landless	—	—	1	20.00
	(ii) Less than 1	—	—	—	—
	(iii) 1-2	3	50.00	2	40.00
	(iv) 2-4	—	—	1	20.00
	(v) 4-10	2	33.33	—	—
	(vi) 10 and above	1	16.67	1	20.00
6.	Annual income (Rs.)				
	(i) Upto 1100	1	16.67	1	20.00
	(ii) 11000-25000	2	33.33	—	—
	(iii) 25000-50000	3	50.00	3	60.00
	(iv) 50000-100000	—	—	—	—
	(v) Above 100000	—	—	1	20.00
7.	No. of Pradhan Living outside villege	—	—	—	—
8.	No. of Pradhan trained under JRY	6	100.00	5	100.00

were agriculturists while in the RM Block, four were agriculturists and one was engaged in milk trading. In the MB block, 3 Pradhans were marginal farmers, 2 had between 4-10 hectares of land and 1 was a landlord as he owned more than 10 hectares of land. In the RM Block, 1 Pradhan was landless. He was the same person who had been promoted to the position of pradhan from the upa-pradhan. Two were having between 2-4 hectares of land and 1 was a landlord here as the land in his possession was more than 10 hectares.

From the point of view of income, one Pradhan in each Block had an income of less than Rs.11000 a year, which means he was living below the poverty line. In the MB Block, 2 Pradhans were having an income of between Rs.10000-25000 and 3 between Rs.25000-50000 a year. In the R.M. Block, also, two Pradhans were also having an income of between Rs. 25000-50000 a year. One Pradhan in this block was having an income of between Rs.50000-100000. It means that comparatively the Pradhans of the R.M. Block were better off than those of the M.B. Block.

In the MB Block all Pradhans were living in their villages while in the RM Block 4 were living in their villages and 1 in the district headquarters Saharanpur, because he was working there as principal of a secondary school. However, occasionally he visited to his village. The people of this Gram Panchayat said that for even a small work they had to run to Saharanpur. Some times they did not find him at his residence. When asked why they had elected him, they said at that time he was not a principal and was living with them. Except for this residential drawback, he had a people - friendly approach for village development, they said.

All the Pradhans of both the blocks had received training about JRY. The training was held at the Block headquarters. It may be mentioned here that when the Pradhans were asked about this training, except one Pradhan of Shambalhari GP of the R.M. Block, all of them denied having been given any training about JRY. On verification from the Block and DRDA offices, it was found that all the Pradhans had in fact undergone training. When confronted with this evidence they told us that they had only attended meetings at the Block headquarters. However, it was confirmed from both the sides that in the training more time was spent on discussing the problems of the villages than on discussing the technical and non-technical problems the Pradhans had been encounting in implementation of the scheme.

Table 4.2 presents the size and social composition of the GPs. It shows that the average number of villages per GP in the MB block was 2.3 as against 1.4 in the RM Block. It means the former had more villages per GP than the latter. In the MB block about 48 per cent of the total members of the GP were from the SC category and the rest were from the other categories. Further, among SC members about 36 per cent were males and 12 per cent were females. Among the others about 42 per cent were males and about 10 per cent were females. This distribution shows that participation of women belonging to the SCs is more than that of non - SC women in panchayat affairs. In the case of the RM Block 36 per cent of the total GP members were from the SCs and 64 per cent were from the other categories. Among the SCs about 27 per cent were men and about 9 per cent were women. In case of the others 52 per cent were males and 12 per cent were females. Thus, in this Block the situation was entirely different from the M.B. Block. In the former, SC participation in village affairs was more prominent than in the latter.

The position as regards the share of the SCs and the others in the total population as well as the level of both male and female literacy has been depicted in Table 4.3. In the MB Block the SC population in the sampled villages ranges from 21 per cent to about 60 per cent. As against this in the sampled villages in the RM Block, their population ranges from about 21 to 42 per cent. This explains why the share of the SCs in the membership of the GP was higher in the MB Block than in the RM Block. The male and female literacy rates are the highest in Halwana GP of the MB block, where the male literacy was 47 per cent and the female literacy was 28 per cent and the lowest in Nagal Mafi GP where it is 30 and 6 per cent respectively. Two factors may be responsible for this phenomenon: one, the former village is situated near a town whereas the latter is situated far from any urban centre. Second, the latter was dominated by the

Table 4.2 : Size and Composition of the Gram Panchayats

S.No.	Name of Panchayats	No. of Villages in a panchayat	SC		Others		Grand Total
			Male	Female	Male	Female	
1	2	3	4	5	6	7	8
	M.B. Block						
1.	Nagal Mafi	2	6 (50.00)	3 (25.00)	— (25.00)	12 —	(100.00)
2.	Halwana	3	4 (28.57)	2 (14.28)	7 (50.00)	1 (7.14)	14 (100.00)
3.	M.Bad	3	8 (42.10)	2 (10.53)	72 (36.81)	19 (10.53)	(100.00)
4.	Khurampur	1	3 (21.43)	1 (7.14)	8 (57.15)	7 (14.28)	14 (100.00)
5.	Khusalipur	2	4 (23.54)	2 (11.76)	10 (58.82)	1 (5.88)	7 (100.00)
6.	Talhapur	3	6 (50.00)	1 (8.33)	2 (16.67)	3 (25.00)	12 (100.00)
	Total		31 (36.05)	11 (12.50)	37 (42.05)	9 (10.23)	88 (100.00)
	R.M. Block						
1.	Ghatra	1	3 (17.65)	2 (11.76)	11 (64.71)	1 (5.88)	17 (100.00)
2.	Sambhal Heri	1	4 (23.53)	1 (5.88)	9 (52.94)	3 (17.65)	17 (100.00)
3.	Sakatpur	2	4 (33.33)	1 (8.33)	5 (41.67)	2 (16.67)	12 (100.00)
4.	Niwada	2	5 (38.46)	2 (15.38)	5 (38.47)	1 (7.09)	13 (100.00)
5.	Umahi Kalan	1	4 (25.00)	1 (6.25)	9 (56.25)	2 (12.50)	16 (100.00)
	TOTAL		20 (26.67)	7 (9.33)	39 (52.00)	9 (12.00)	75 (100.00)

Table 4.3 : Social Composition of the Population of Panchayats (based on 1991 Census)

S. No.	Name of Panchayats	SC (%)	Others (%)	Total (%)	Literacy Rate	
					Male(%)	Female (%)
1	2	3	4	5	6	7
	M.B. Block					
1.	Nagal Mafi	62.17	37.83	100.00	30	6
2.	Halwana	44.27	55.73	100.00	47	28
3.	M.Bad	21.85	78.15	100.00	44	13
4.	Khurampur	21.12	78.88	100.00	46	23
5.	Khusalipur	22.24	77.76	100.00	44	11
6.	Talhapur	26.31	73.69	100.00	32	10
	R.M. Block					
1.	Ghatra	21.57	78.43	100.00	51	16
2.	Sambhal Heri	24.59	75.41	100.00	48	31
3.	Sakatpur	30.41	69.59	100.00	40	12
4.	Niwada	41.59	58.41	100.00	49	36
5.	Umahi Kalan	40.91	59.09	100.00	63	64

SC population while the former was not. In the RM Block, the highest literacy rate among both males and females was in Umahi kalan GP as the Table shows. Here, it is interesting to note that the female literacy rate was higher than that of the males. Facilities for schooling and their utilisation are the main factors responsible for this phenomenon. Besides this the GP is also near the town. The lowest literacy rate among both males and females was found in Sakatpur where among the former it was 40 per cent and among the latter 12 per cent . It is obvious that the residents of this GP were insufficiently oriented towards schooling of their the children. This particular GP consisting of 2 villages, has one primary school which has never had its full complement of teachers. Besides, instead of helping the school, some of the villagers have even grabbed the land belonging to the primary school.

Population Below Poverty Line

Table 4.4 shows the distribution of poverty among the sampled villages. This data has been taken from the village register maintained by the Village Development Officer. The Table shows that the intensity of poverty is higher in the MB block

Table 4.4: Population below poverty li9ne in the Gram Panchayats
(In Percentage)

S. No.	Name of Panchayats	SC	Others	Total
1	2	3	4	5
	M.B. Block			
1.	Nagal Mafi	97.90	54.60	81.52
2.	Halwana	93.91	60.56	75.22
3.	M.Bad	100.00	45.94	60.91
4.	Khurampur	66.59	28.35	36.42
5.	Khusalipur	63.71	39.82	45.13
6.	Talhapur	99.25	49.47	62.56
	R.M. Block			
1.	Ghatra	75.99	35.12	43.94
2.	Sambhal Heri	85.85	41.99	47.24
3.	Sakatpur	78.08	4.59	26.94
4.	Niwada	80.05	30.67	50.62
5.	Umahi Kalan	85.86	34.27	55.37

than in the RM Block. This is natural as the former is more backward than the latter. Poverty in both the blocks is found more among the SCs than the others. In the M.Bad GP of the MB block all the SCs were living below the poverty line. If we look at total population below poverty line, we find that the highest percentage of the population below the poverty line in this Block was in Nagal Mafi GP and the lowest in Khurampur GP. In the RM Block, the extent of poverty was the largest in Umahikalan GP and the lowest in Sakatpur GP. If we look at these levels of poverty along with table 4.3 which shows distribution of population between the SCs and others we find that the population of the SCs and intensity of poverty are directly related.

Details of the GP's Officials

Table 4.5 gives a picture of the officials of the panchayats. None of the GPs in either of the two blocks has a full-time secretary. There is one secretary for every Nyaya Panchayat which consist of about 5 or 6 GPs. Part-time here does not mean that the secretary is employed on a part time basis. He is a full-time state government employee but working with the GPs only part of the time. Since he is a state government employee, the GP does not have any control on him.

Table 4.5: Officials of Panchayats

S. No.	*Particulars*	*M.B. Block*	*R.M. Block*
1	*2*	*3*	*4*
1.	Total No. of Panchayats	6 (100.00)	6 (100.00)
2.	No. of Panchayat having full time secretary	—	—
3.	No. of Panchayat having part time secretary	6 (100)	5 (100)
4.	Othjer Staff Employed		
	(i) Full Time	1 (16.77)	—
	(ii) Part Time	5 (83.33)	5 (100.00

Figures in Parenthesis Show Percentages.

As per the Panchayat GP Act, the GP is empowered to employ any part - time worker for the purpose of its work. In such a case, the salary and other service conditions will be determined by the Panchayat itself. Under this provision, a group of panchayats say 4 or 5 may employ a person on casual basis to assist the Panchayat secretary. Each panchayat shall pay him about Rs.60/- per month. As the table shows, of the GPs in the two Blocks only one GP (M. Bad) has engaged a permanent employee and the rest have engaged only Part time workers. The reasons for this particular GP employing a permanent worker unlike others, are ; (a) this GP has a comparatively larger population, and (b) its financial position is also to some extent more comfortable than that of the others mainly for two reasons; (a) weekly market is held in this village yielding some income from the shopkeepers to the GP and the (b) Block headquarters is also situated in this village because of which some marketing facilities have developed providing additional income to the GP. In a nut shell the level of the socio-economic infrastructure and staff of a panchayat depends on its financial position.

About the staffing arrangement for the GPs, it may be mentioned that the strength of their staff has remained unaffected by the launching of the JRY. After the launching of the scheme the work of the panchayat secretary has increased. It is therefore necessary to increase the strength of the GP staff. This has become all the important after the 73rd Constitutional Amendment which has added to the GP's responsibilities.

Summing Up

The above discussion may be summed up as follows: None of the Pradhans from the Sampled Panchayats belongs to the SCs and there is also no woman among them. All the Pradhans except one own land with. Some of them even being landlords. The one landless Pradhan was earlier an Upa-Pradhan but when the Pradhan became the Pramukh of the Kshetra Panchayat he was promoted as Pradhan. The population of the SCs was comparatively high in the M.B Block. The intensity of poverty was found to be more in the MB, Block and it was directly related to the strength of its SC population. Of the total Pradhans two were living the below poverty line keeping in view Rs. 11000/- per annum income as the criterion. None of the Panchayats was having a it full-time secretary and only one panchayat of the M.B. was having full time employee while the rest had had only part time employees.

5

INCOME AND EXPENDITURE OF THE SAMPLED PANCHAYATS

Introduction

In this chapter income of the GPs source - wise, and their expenditure under the JRY with its wage - non-wage ratio are discussed.

Source wise Income of the Sampled Panchayats

Table 5.1 shows the income of the sampled panchayats together with its sources for a period of three years. Let us first take the GPs in the MB block. Here, during 1990-91, of the total income of the panchayats 36.70, 42.93 and 20.3 per cent had been collected from taxes, own enterprises and assets and share of land revenue respectively. During 1991-92, the income sourcewise in a same order was 35.37, 45.13 and 19.14 per cent respectively. During 1992-93, the contribution of the different sources in the same sequence was 47.87, 34.43 and 17.70 respectively. Thus, according to the data for the first two years the share of taxes in the total income of the panchayats was about one third. But during 1992-93, it rose to about forty per cent. This is a healthy sign. The income from own enterprises, including sale of their products etc during the first two years was about 43 and 45 per cent respectively, which was reduced to about 34 per cent during 1992-93. The share of land revenue in the total income during

Table 5.1: Source-Wise Income of the Panchayats

S. No.	*Sources*	*M.B. Block*			*R.M. Block*		
		1990-91	*1991-92*	*1992-93*	*1990-91*	*1991-92*	*1992-93*
1	2	*3*	*4*	*5*	*6*	*7*	*8*
1.	Taxes	55910.50	60910.50	75682.50	10765.00	10765.00	10765.00
		(36.70)	(35.73)	(47.87)	(15.51)	(13.26)	(12.95)
2.	Own Enterprises/Assets	65410.00	76950.00	54419.00	30232.00	31663.00	36848.00
	or sale of product	(42.93)	(45.13)	(34.43)	(43.71)	(39.01)	(44.30)
3.	Share of land	31040.00	32629.00	27985.00	28301.00	38743.00	35476.00
	Revenue	(20.3)	(19.14)	(17.70)	(40.78)	(44.73)	(42.25)
	Grant or Untied Fund	—	—	—	—	—	—
	Loan from Govt.	—	—	—	—	—	—
	Donation	—	—	—	—	—	—
	Other Income	—	—	—	—	—	—
4.	Total Income (1 to 3)	152360.50	170489.50	158086.50	69398.00	81171.00	83089.00
		(100.00)	(100.00)	(100.00)	(100.00)	(100.00)	(100.00)
5.	Average Income per Panchayat	25393.42	28414.83	26347.75	13879.60	16234.20	17017.80
6.	Allocation of Fund under JRY	453446.00	314709.21	475676.00	312418.00	235824.00	347402.00
7.	Ratio of JRY Fund to total resources of the Pachayats (%)	75.85	64.86	75.06	81.82	74.39	80.14
8.	Total Resources (4 & 6)	605806.50	483198.71	633762.50	381816.00	316995.00	433491.00
9.	Average Income(including JRY) per Panchayat	100967.75	80866.45	105627.08	76363.20	63399.00	86698.20

Figures in Parentheses are percentages. *Source* : Compiled from the DRDA Office, Saharanpur

the three years has also shown a steadly decline. This may be due to two reasons: (a) due to the division of land holdings most of the holdings have become sub marginal where land revenue has not been imposed and (b) ineffective collection of the total land revenue during the reference period. The average income (excluding JRY allocation) per panchayat during 1990-91,1991-92 and 1992-93 has been Rs. 25393.42, Rs.28414.83 and Rs. 26347.50 respectively. This figure after including the funds allocated to Panchayats through JRY has been jumped to 100967.75, Rs. 80866.45 and Rs. 105627.08, respectively. It means that the share of the JRY funds in the total income of the Panchayats has been 75.85, 64.86 and 75.86 per cent in the three years respectively.

In the R.M. Block, the situation is different from that in the M.B. Block. In this Block, the share of taxes to the total income of the panchayats was about 16 per cent in 1990-91 and about 13 per cent in 1991-92. In 1992-93 although in the MB Block it was as high as 47.87 per cent in this that is the RM Block it was as low as about 13 per cent. Secondly in the M.B Block it has shown an upward trend as against a declining trend in the RM Block. The income from own enterprises/ assets in the R.M. Block has been steady at around 40 per cent and almost at par with the ratios for the MB Block. It may be noted here that the share of land revenue in the total income in the RM Block is more than 40 per cent which is just about double of the share of this source in the panchayat income in the MB Block. This is natural because this block is more developed than the M.B. Block. Also here the average size of the holdings is higher than in the M.B. Block.

The average income per Panchayat excluding JRY allocation in the RM block has been about Rs. 13880, Rs. 16234 and Rs. 17018 during 1990-91, 1991-92 and 1992-93 respectively which has been lower than that of the other Panchayats in the other Block. The average income per panchayat in the RM Block after including the funds allocated under JRY jumped to Rs. 76363.20, Rs. 63399.00 and Rs. 86698.20 respectively. This shows the ratio of JRY funds to the total income of the panchayats at 81.82, 74.39 and and 80.14 per cent in 1990-91, 1991-92 and 1992-93 respectively. It means that about 75 per cent of the total resources of the panchayats in this Block have been contributed by this scheme. In other words, we can say JRY has meant PRIs.

During the course of the survey and after meeting the pradhans, panchayat secretaries, block, DRDA and ZP officials it has been revealed that the house tax which is a cess on the land revenue, has neither been sincerely levied by the panchayats nor has been paid by the villagers on their own. However, the panchayat records show that it has been paid. Actually, the villagers have paid this tax only when they have wanted to contest any election. Most of the panchayats show this tax as 'Sharamdan' done by the payer while the 'Sharamdan' has in fact not been done. In the M.B. Block, the Assistant Block Development Officer (Panchayat) said in the presence of the Block Development Officer that when he was a secretary sometime back he and the Pradhans used to pay some part of this tax from their own pockets and showed some as having been paid through 'Sharamdan' to complete the tax register.

The reason for not collecting this tax as disclosed by the Pradhans was that they did not want to become unpopular in the village and did not want to displease their voters. But the real reason was unwillingness on the part of the Panchayats to collect it even though the villagers had sufficient purchasing power to pay it. The second reason was the nature of this tax itself as it has been left at the discretion of the panchayats to levy it. The remedy lies in making this tax compulsory imposed by panchayats.

It may be appropriate to throw some light on the income of the Zilla Panchayat (ZP) of Saharanpur district. In this district, during 1993-94. of the total income of the ZP, more than 37 per cent has been mobilized through taxes and non tax measures. This self-raised income of the ZP constitutes about 12 per cent of the district sector outlay under the district planning. But this amount has not been integrated either with the plan of the district nor with the JRY Scheme.

Expenditure Under JRY

Table 5.2 shows the allocation and expenditure under JRY during the three years 1990-91 to 1992-93.

To find out how much of the total allocation under the scheme has been spent, the ratio of the expenditure to the total allocation has been worked out. This ratio shows that in the MB block, of the total allocation more than 95 per cent

Table 5.2: Allocation and Expenditure under JRY

S. No.	*Particulars*	*M.B. Block*			*R.M. Block*		
		1990-91	*1991-92*	*1992-93*	*1990-91*	*1991-92*	*1992-93*
1	*2*	*3*	*4*	*5*	*6*	*7*	*8*
1.	Total Allocation under JRY (Rs.)	453446.00	314709.21	475676.00	312418.00	235824.00	347402.00
2.	Total Expenditure (Rs.)	446291.00	286597.00	475676.00	312016.00	234782.50	346447.00
3.	Wage component (%)	40.09	38.57	37.71	43.79	58.13	43.84
4.	Non-wage component (%)	59.91	61.43	62.29	56.21	41.87	56.16
5.	Expenditure on food grains (%)	—	—	—	—	—	—
6.	Cash Expenditure (%)	100.00	100.00	100.00	100.00	100.00	100.00
7.	Average Expenditure per Panchayat (Rs.)	74381.83	47766.17	82746.00	62403.20	46956.40	69289.40

Figures in Parentheses are percentages.
Source : Compiled from the DRDA Office, Saharanpur.

has been spent, whereas in the R.M. Block, almost all allocated funds have been spent. It means in the latter Block the unspent balance is nil.

About the wage component, the JRY guidelines say that atleast 60 per cent of the JRY allocation must be spent as wage component. But in the implementation of the JRY in the sampled Blocks, these guidelines have not been adhered to. What we want to stress is that all the officials and non-officials we contacted said in chorus that the wage and non wage condition must be relaxed. It may be left to the Panchayats to utilise the earmarked resources keeping the ground realties in view.

As per the JRY guidelines a part of the wage should be given the form of food grains. But this has not been done in the sampled villages as it is not fashionable to take grain as a part of the wages. Moreover this has not been a food grain scarcity area. Here, foodgrains are available throughout the year. Therefore, wages to the workers have been given in cash only. The average expenditure per panchayat has also been worked out which shows that the GPs under the MB Block have incurred more expenditure per Panchayat than those of the RM Block.

Summing Up

It has been seen that in the case of the M.B. Block, of the total income (excluding JRY) of the Panchayats, about 40 per cent have been contributed by taxes. As against this in the R.M. Block it was found that not even 20 per cent of the total income of the Panchayats has come from this source. The JRY funds to the total income of the Panchayats have been about 75 per cent in the R.M. Block. Of the total JRY allocation, about 95 per cent has been spent in the M.B. Block. With a few exceptions the JRY guidelines that at least 60 per cent of the allocation will be spent on wage has not been followed in the sampled GPs. No part of the JRY expenditure has been incurred on giving foodgrains as part of the workers' wages.

6

SOCIO-ECONOMIC CHARACTERISTICS OF THE BENEFICIARIES

Introduction

In this chapter, the size and composition of the beneficiaries along with their occupational structure, educational level, dwelling status, income, per capita expenditure and other related aspects are dealt with. It may be mentioned that the beneficiaries studied are those who had got employment in activities connected with the creation of assets in the sampled villages, in other words, those who had benefited from the JRY. The SCs/STs, weaker sections and farmers who have benefited from the IAY and the MWS form part of separate chapters.

Size and Composition of the Beneficiaries

Table 6.1 shows the size and composition of the sampled beneficiaries who took employment in various activities carried out under the JRY by the Panchayats.

In the M.B. Block, the total number of the beneficiaries was 149 of whom 71.14 per cent (106) were SCs and 28.86 per cent (43) were others (non SCs). There are no STs in this district. Hence they have not found a place among the beneficiaries. It may be mentioned that the total number of the beneficiaries interviewed was 150 but one beneficiary has not been included in the analysis as he had not done any work

Table 6.1: Size and Composition of the Beneficiaries

Classification	M.B. Block				R.M. Block			
	1990-91	1991-92	1992-93	Total	1990-91	1991-92	1992-93	Total
Total	48 (32.21)	48 (32.21)	53 (35.57)	149 (100)	49 (32.67)	50 (33.33)	51 (34.00)	150 (100.00)
S.C.	36 (33.96)	34 (32.08)	36 (33.96)	106 (100.00)	33 (32.04)	32 (31.08)	38 (36.89)	103 (100.00)
Other	12 (27.91)	14 (32.56)	17 (39.53)	43 (100.00)	16 (34.04)	18 (38.30)	13 (27.66)	47 (100.00)
Women	3 (33.33)	2 (22.22)	4 (44.44)	9 (100.00)	—	—	—	—
Landless	24 (32.43)	24 (32.43)	26 (35.14)	74 (100.00)	38 (34.23)	36 (32.43)	37 (33.33)	111 (100.00)

Figures in Parentheses are percentages.

but had figured in the record of the wage earners under the scheme.

The beneficiaries are further classified as women and landless workers. On this basis 6.04 per cent (9) were women and 49.66 per cent (74) were landless. The SC beneficiaries were found to have figured almost equally in all the three years. The number of other beneficiaries was 43, of whom the percentages during 1990-91, 1991-92 and 1992-93 were about 28, 33 and 40 respectively. Of the total women beneficiaries the corresponding percentages were about 33, 22 and 44 were during in the three years respectively. Of the total 74 landless workers, the spread was almost equalat about one third in all the three years.

In the R.M. Block, of the total 150 beneficiaries about 69 per cent (103) were from the SCs and about 31 per cent (47) from other communities. The beneficiaries were equally spread over all the three years. Of the total SCs, 32.04, 31.08 and 36.89 per cents were spread over 1990-91, 1991-92 and 1992-93 respectively. Of the other category of the beneficiaries, 34.04, 38.30 and 27.66 per cents respectively figured in the three years. As the Table shows the landless workers were spread equally over all the three years. There was no women beneficiary in this Block.

Three conclusions emerged from the above discussion:

(a) Of the total employment opportunities about 70 per cent are taken by the SCs in both the Blocks.

(b) Of the total beneficiaries about three fourth are landless in the R.M. Block. They constitute about 50 per cent in the M.B. Block.

(c) Women who are supposed to be 30 per cent of the total beneficiaries, are merely 6 per cent and that too only in the M.B. Block. No women took employment under the scheme in the R.M. Block.

Table 6.2 presents the age classification of the sampled beneficiaries. It shows that in the M.B. Block, of the total beneficiaries, 17.45 per cent are in the age group of 16-25, 36.91 per cent in the age group of 26-35, 24.83 per cent in the age group of 36-45, 15.44 per cent in the age group of 46.58 and 5.37 per cent in the age group of 59 and above. It means no child was engaged under the scheme but it is surprising

Table 6.2: Age Classification of the Beneficiaries

Classification Beneficiaries	M.B. Block						R.M. Block					
	16-25	*26-35*	*36-45*	*46-58*	*59 & above*	*Total*	*16-25*	*26-35*	*36-45*	*46-58*	*59 & above*	*Total*
Total	26 (17.45)	55 (36.91)	37 (24.83)	23 (15.44)	8 (5.37)	149 (100.00)	42 (28.00)	41 (27.33)	23 (15.33)	33 (22.00)	11 (7.33)	150 (100.00)
S.C.	17 (16.04)	39 (36.79)	29 (27.36)	14 (13.21)	7 (6.60)	106 (100.00)	34 (33.00)	36 (34.95)	9 (8.74)	17 (16.50)	7 (6.80)	103 (100.00)
Other	9 (20.93)	16 (37.21)	8 (18.60)	9 (20.93)	1 (2.33)	43 (100.00)	8 (10.81)	5 (10.64)	14 (29.79)	16 (34.04)	4 (8.51)	47 (100.00)
Women	— —	2 (22.22)	4 (44.44)	1 (11.11)	2 (22.22)	9 (100.00)	—	—	—	—	—	—
Landless	22 (29.73)	31 (41.89)	14 (18.92)	7 (9.46)	— —	74 (100.00)	40 (36.04)	32 (28.83)	15 (13.51)	14 (12.61)	10 (9.00)	111 (100.00)

Figures in Parentheses show the percentages.

that about 6 per cent of the total workers were aged citizen. Now let us see the categorywise distribution pattern of the beneficiarics. In the case of the SCs, the highest number of the beneficiaries were in the age group of 26-35 followed by the 36-45 age group and the lowest were in the age group of 59 and above. A similar pattern can be observed in the case of the category of others of the working population. In the case of women it is astonishing to note that although their total number was only 9 even as many 22.22 per cent were in the age group of 59 and above. It shows the compulsive necessity on their part to earn to augment the income of their families. No woman was in the age group of 16-25 as a worker under the JRY. In the landless category, the highest number were in the age group of 26-35 and the lowest were in that of 46-58. There was no worker from amongst them in the age group of 59 and above.

In the R.M. Block of the total beneficiaries, 28 per cent were in the an age group of 16-25, 27.33 per cent in the age group of 26-35, 15.33 were per cent in the age group of 36-45, 22.00 were per cent in the age group of 46-58 and 7.33 per cent were in the age group of 59 and above. If we compare this age group pattern of the RM Block with that of its counter part in the MB Block, we find that in the R.M. Block the distribution pattern is more or less uniform. In the case of the SCs the highest number of the beneficiaries were in the age group of 16-35 followed by the age group of 16-25 and the lowest number were in the age group of 59 and above. In the case of the other categories of the workers, the highest number were in the age group of 46-58 followed by the age group of 36-45 and the lowest were in the age group of 59 and above. There were no women beneficiaries in this Block. In the case of the landless, the highest number were in the age group of 16-25 followed by the age group of 26-35 and the lowest were in the age group of 59 and above.

If we compare the two age group patterns of the beneficiaries in the Blocks we find both similarities and dissimilarities. The lowest number in both the Blocks are in the age group of 59 and above and immediately above that in the age group of 46-58. Secondly in the case of the SCs the highest number in both the Blocks were in the age group of 16-35. The dissimilarities are: (a) the beneficiaries in the age group of 59 and above are more in the R.M. Block than in the MB Block (b) In the case of the other categories the highest number in the MB Block were in the age group of 26-35 while in the R.M. Block they were from the 46-58 age group (c): in the case of the landless in the M.B. Block the highest number were in the age group of 26-35 as against the age group of 16-25 in the R.M. Block.

Occupational Structure of the Sampled Beneficiaries:

Table 6.3 presents the occupational structure of the sampled beneficiaries. The beneficiaries have been classified into four occupational group viz., landless workers, marginal farmers, small farmers and artisans. These occupational groups are also categorized into the SCs and the non SCs.

Table 6.3: Occupational Structure of the Beneficiaries

Social Classi-cation	*Landless*	*Marginal Farmers*	*Small Farmers*	*Artisans*	*Total*
1	*2*	*3*	*4*	*5*	*6*
M.B. B.lock					
Total	70 (46.98)	67 (44.97)	8 (5.37)	4 (2.68)	149 (100.00)
SC	54 (50.94)	48 (45.28)	3 (2.83)	1 (0.94)	106 (100.00)
Others	16 (37.21)	19 (44.19)	5 (11.63)	3 (6.98)	43 (100.00)
R.M. Block					
Total	112 (74.67)	38 (25.33)	—	—	150 (100.00)
SC	75 (72.82)	28 (27.18)			103 (100.00)
Others	37 (78.72)	10 (21.13)			47 (100.00)

Figures in Parenthesis show the percentage.

In the M.B. Block, of the total beneficiaries, 46.98 per cent were landless workers, 44.97 per cent were marginal farmers, 5.37 per cent were small farmers and the rest 2.68 per cent were artisans. It means that more than 90 per cent of the workers were either landless or marginal farmers and not even 10 per cent comprised of small farmers and artisans. It may be noted here that artisans who are supposed to undertake skill oriented activities are also sometimes forced to work as wage earner as their crafts are vanishing day by day. Although their percentage is only about 3 per cent, this is an undesirable trend which needs to be checked.

Looking at the occupational pattern groupwise, we find the following picture:

(a) Of the total SC beneficiaries in the MB Block 50.94 per cent were landless workers, 45.28 per cent were marginal farmers, 2.83 per cent were small farmers and about 1 per cent were artisans. In other words, almost all workers were either landless or marginal farmers.

(b) In the case of the other categories 37.21 per cent of the total were landless workers, 44.19 per cent were marginal farmers, 11.63 per cent were small farmers and 6.98 per cent were artisans. It means almost all the small farmer and artisan beneficiaries were from the other categories of the workers.

In the R.M. Block, of the total beneficiaries, 74.67 per cent were landless workers and 25.33 per cent were marginal farmers. There was none from amongst the small farmers and artisans. Of the SCs beneficiaries 72.82 per cent were landless and the rest are marginal farmers. In the case of the other categories 78.72 per cent were landless and 21.13 per cent belonged to the marginal farmer category.

After comparing the occupational structure of the beneficiaries in the two Blocks we find that in the M.B. Block about 47 per cent and 45 per cent were from the landless and marginal farmer categories respectively, in their comparable percentage for the R.M. Block at about 75 and 25 respectively. An almost similar trend can also be noticed from the social classification of the SC and Non-SC beneficiaries. In the R.M. Block, there was no SC worker from amongst the small farmers and artisans whereas in the M.B. Block, more than 8 per cent of the total workers were from these two categories. It clearly shows that due to poverty, the small farmers and artisans in the M.B. Block are also compelled to takeup wage employment whereas in the other Block they have no such compulsion.

The position as regards the number of the beneficiaries per household in the various social groups can be seen from

Table 6.4: Wage Employment Pattern of the Sampled Beneficiaries

Classification of the Beneficiaries	*M.B. Block*					*R.M. Block*				
	Wage Employment Status of Households				*Total*	*Wage Employment Status of Households*				*Total*
	1	2	3	4	*Total*	*1*	2	3	4	*Total*
Total	136 (91.57)	10 (6.71)	3 (2.01)	—	149 (100.00)	136 (90.67)	11 (7.33)	3 (2.00)	—	150 (100.00)
S.C.	96 (90.57)	7 (6.60)	3 (2.83)	—	106 (100.00)	95 (92.23)	8 (7.77)	—	—	103 (100.00)
Others	40 (93.02)	3 (6.98)	—	—	43 (100.00)	41 (87.23)	3 (6.38)	3 (6.38)	—	47 (100.00)
Women	—	6 (66.67)	3 (33.33)	—	9 (100.00)	—	—	—	—	—
Landless	70 (94.59)	4 (5.41)	—	—	74 (100.00)	97 (87.39)	11 (9.91)	3 (2.70)	—	111 (100.00)

Figures in Parentheses show the percentages.

Table 6.4. In the M.B. Block, of the total worker households, 91.27 per cent were having only one wage earner, 6.71 per cent two wage earners and 2.01 per cent 3 wage earners. It means that more than 90 per cent of the poverty stricken households were having only one wage earner. In the case of the SC households, 90.57 per cent were having only one wage earner, 6.60 per cent 2 wage earners and 2.83 per cent 3 wage earners. In the case of the other categories of the total worker households, 93.02 per cent were having only 1 wage earner and 6.98 per cent 2 wage earners with no household having 3 wage earners. In case of the households whose women were worked as wage earners under the JRY, 66.67 per cent of the total were having 2 wage earners and the rest 33.33 per cent were having 3 wage earners as the table shows. In the case of the landless worker households, 94.57 per cent of the total were having only 1 wage earner and 5.41 2 wage earners.

In the R.M. Block, at the aggregate level of the total, 90.67 per cent household were having only 1 wage earner, 7.33 per cent 2 wage earners and 2 per cent 3 wage earners. In the case of the SC households, 92.23 per cent of the total were having only 1 wage earner and 7.77 per cent were having 2 wage earners. In the case of the other categories of the total worker households, 87.23 per cent were having only 1 wage earner, 6.38 were having 2 wage earners and the same percentage were having 3 wage earners in these households.

To conclude, at the aggregate level, the pattern of the wage earners households is almost the same in both the Blocks. When we come to the SC level, we find that there was no household having 3 wage earners in the R.M. Block whereas M.B. Block has. In the case of the landless workers, in the R.M. Block, about 3 per cent households were having 3 wage earners whereas in the M.B. Block no landless household was having this number of wage earners.

Dwelling Status of the Sampled Beneficiaries

Table 6.5 presents the dwelling status of the sampled beneficiaries. The dwellings of the workers were classified into kachha house, pacca house and semi pacca house. Let us discuss the position Block-wise.

In the M.B. Block, of the total beneficiaries, 71.81 per cent were having kachha houses, 27.52 pacca houses and 0.67 per

Table 6.5: Dwelling Status of the Beneficiaries

Beneficiaries Category	*M.B. Block*				*R.M. Block*			
	Kachha House	*Pacca House*	*Semi Pacca House*	*Total*	*Kachha*	*Pacca House*	*Semi Pacca House*	*Total*
Total	107	41	1	149	97	35	18	150
	(71.81)	(27.52)	(0.67)	(100.00)	(64.97)	(23.33)	(12.00)	(100.00)
S.C.	77	28	1	106	63	17	6	86
	(72.64)	(26.42)	(0.94)	(100.00)	(73.26)	(19.77)	(6.98)	(100.00)
Others	30	13	—	43	34	18	12	64
	(69.77)	(30.23)		(100.00)	(53.13)	(28.13)	(18.75)	(100.00)
Women	3	6	—	9	—	—	—	—
	(33.33)	(66.67)		(100.00)				(100.00)
Landless	63	10	1	74	66	33	12	111
	(85.14)	(13.51)	(1.35)	(100.00)	(59.46)	(29.73)	(10.81)	(100.00)

Figures in Parentheses show the percentages.

cent semi-pacca houses. A house having either wall or roof made of pacca material is called semi-pacca. Of the total SC workers, 72.64 per cent were having kachha houses and 26.42 per cent pacca houses. In the case of the other categories of workers, 69.77 per cent were having kachha houses and 30.23 per cent pacca houses. None of the workers in the others, category was having semi pacca house as the table shows. In the case of the households, from which women get employment under the scheme about 33 per cent of the total were having kachha houses and the rest were having pacca houses and none semi-pacca house. In the case of the landless workers, 85.14 per cent of the total were having kachha houses, 13.51 pacca houses and a little more than 1 per cent semi-pacca houses. The table clearly shows that the SC and landless beneficiaries had a larger percentage of kachha houses than the 'others' category of the workers. However in the case of the households from where women beneficiaries were drawn about 67 per cent had pacca houses. This is the highest among all the categories of the workers.

In the R.M. Block, of the total households, 64.67, 23.33 and 12.00 per cent were having kachha, pacca and semi-pacca houses respectively. In the case of the SCs, the corresponding percentages were 73.26, 19.77 and 6.98. In the case of the 'others', the percentages were 53.13 28.13 and 18.75 respectively. In the case of the landless workers, 59.46 per cent, 29.73 per cent and 10.81 per cent of the total workers were having kachha, pacca and semi pacca houses respectively.

If we compare the dwelling status of the beneficiaries in both the Blocks, we can draw the following conclusions:

(a) At the aggregate level, the workers in the MB Block were having more kachha houses than those in the R.M. Block;

(b) In the case of the SCs, the dwelling unit status was almost the same in both the Blocks while in the case of the others category the status of those in the R.M. Block was better than that of their counterpart in the M.B. Block; and

(c) In the case of the landless workers, those of the R.M. Block were better placed than their brethren in the M.B. Block as the percentage of kachha householders among them was about 57 per cent as against about 85 per cent in the latter.

Educational Level of the Sampled Workers

The educational standard of the sampled beneficiaries is depicted in table 6.6. The beneficiaries have been classified into seven categories, namely, illiterate, literate, primary, middle, high school, intermediate and graduate and above.

In the M.B. Block, 40.24, 12.75, 21.48, 16.11 and 8.72 per cent of the total beneficiaries were illiterate, literate and of primary, middle and high school level standards respectively. In the case of the SCs, 41.51 per cent of the total were illiterate, 13.21 were literate, 18.87 per cent were educated upto the 5th standard, 16.07 per cent upto the 8th standard and 10.38 per cent had studied upto high school. In the category of 'others', 39.53 per cent were illiterate, 11.63 per cent were literate, 27.91 per cent had studied upto the 5th standard, 16.28 upto the middle standard and the rest upto high school. All Women worker were found to be illiterate. In the case of the landless workers, 39.19 per cent were illiterate, 9.46 were literate, 24.32 per cent had attained the primary level, 14.86 the middle standard and the rest had studied up to high school. The Table clearly shows that leaving aside women, all of whom were illiterate, about 40 per cent of the total SC, 'others' and the landless beneficiaries in this Block were illiterate. They are followed by those who had studies up to the primary standard. There was nobody among the workers in this Block to have reached the intermediate or graduation level.

In the R.M. Block, 58.67 per cent of the total workers were illiterate, 12.00 per cent were literate, 6.67 per cent had studied up to the primary standard, an equal percentage had reached the middle standard, 9.33 per cent the high school standard, 4.67 per cent the intermediate standard and 2.00 per cent had graduated. Looking at the educational level of the different categories of the workers, we find the following picture.

Of the total SC beneficiaries 65.05 per cent were illiterate, 4.85 were literate, 5.83 per cent had studied up to the primary standard, 6.80 per cent up to the high school standard and

Table 6.6: Educational Level of Beneficiaries

Beneficiaries Category	*Illiterate*	*Literate*	*Primary*	*Middle*	*High School*	*Intermediate*	*Graduate & above*	*Total*
M.B. Block								
Total	*61* (40.24)	*19* (12.75)	*32* (21.48)	*24* (16.11)	*13* (8.72)	—	—	*149* (100.00)
SC	44 (41.51)	14 (13.21)	20 (18.87)	17 (16.07)	11 (10.38)	—	—	106 (100.00)
Others	17 (39.53)	5 (11.63)	12 (27.91)	7 (16.28)	2 (4.65)	—	—	43 (100.00)
Women	9 (100.00)	—	—	—	—	—	—	9 (100.00)
Landless	29 (39.19)	7 (9.46)	18 (24.32)	11 (14.86)	9 (12.16)	—	—	74 (100.00)
R.M. Block								
Total	88 (58.67)	18 (12.00)	10 (6.67)	10 (6.67)	14 (9.33)	7 (4.67)	3 (2.00)	150 (100.00)
SC	67 (65.05)	5 (4.85)	6 (5.83)	7 (6.80)	8 (7.77)	7 (6.80)	3 (2.91)	103 (100.00)
Others	21 (44.68)	13 (27.66)	4 (8.51)	3 (6.38)	6 (12.77)	—	—	47 (100.00)
Women	—	—	—	—	—	—	—	—
Landless	55 (49.55)	16 (14.41)	10 (9.00)	10 (9.00)	13 (11.71)	6 (5.41)	1 (0.90)	111 (100.00)

Figures in Parentheses show the percentages.

6.80 per cent up to the intermediate standard while 2.91 per cent were graduates. In the case of the 'others', 44.68 per cent of the total were illiterate, 27.66 per cent were literate, 8.51 per cent had studied up to the primary standard, 6.38 per cent up to the middle standard and 12.77 per cent up to the high school standard. In this category, none of the beneficiary was either intermediate or graduate. In the case of the landless workers, 49.55 per cent of th total were illiterate, 14.41 per cent were literate, 9.00 per cent each had attained the primary and middle standards, 11.71 per cent the high school standard and 5.41 per cent the intermediate standard. Here also, none was a graduate. This analysis shows that the workers of all the categories in this Block had more illiterates followed by literates among them then those with middle and higher levels of education.

If we compare the educational levels of the beneficiaries in the two blocks we find that (a) the illiterate workers in the R.M. Block were more in number then in the M.B. Block. (b) In the M.B. Block no worker had attained the intermediate or graduation levels while in the R.M. Block about 7 per cent of the workers had reached this level.

Income Profile of the Beneficiaries

Table 6.7 shows the break-up of the beneficiaries in both the Blocks according to Income Groups to which they belonged. They are classified into five income groups. These serially from 1 to 4 are the same as have been classified by the DRDA of Saharanpur in its action Plan for IRDP for 1994-95 based

Table 6.7: Percentage Distribution of the Beneficiaries according to income group

Income Classification (Rs.)	*M.B. Block*			*R.M. Block*		
	1990-91	*1991-92*	*1992-93*	*1990-91*	*1991-92*	*1992-93*
Below 4000	8.16	2.08	—	4.08	2.00	—
4000-6000	26.53	25.00	13.46	44.90	26.00	9.80
6000-8500	32.65	29.17	26.92	20.41	34.00	13.14
8500-11000	14.29	22.92	25.00	18.37	18.00	15.69
11000 & above	18.37	20.83	34.62	12.24	20.00	31.37

on the village wise survey conducted in 1992. The groups are : households having incomes of (1) less than Rs. 4000,(2) Rs. 4000 - Rs. 6000, (3) Rs. 6000 - Rs. 8500 and (4) Rs. 8500 - Rs. 11000. These have been were designated as destitutes, very very poor, very poor and poor respectively.

In the M.B. Block of the total beneficiaries during 1990-91, 8.16 per cent were destitutes, 26.53 per cent were very very poor, 32.65 per cent were very poor and 14.29 per cent were poor. More than 18 per cent were above the poverty line as their income was more than Rs. 11,000.00. During 1991-92, the destitutes were about 75 per cent less than in previous year. The very very poor were about 6 per cent less the very poor about 11 per cent less and the poor about 60 per cent more than in the previous year. Those having income of more than Rs 11000 also were 13 per cent more than in the previous year. During 1992-93, there was no worker having income of less than Rs 4000.00 while those with incomes of between Rs 4000 and Rs. 6000 were about 46 per cent less than in the previous year. The workers having incomes ranging from Rs 6000 to 8500 were about 8 per cent more than in the previous years and those were having income of more than Rs. 11000.00 were about 66 per cent more in this year than in preceding year.

In the R.M. Block the income profile of the workers was like as follows: During 1990-91, 4.08 per cent of the workers were having income below Rs. 4000.00. The percentage of those with income between Rs. 4000 - Rs. 6000 was 44.80 while 20.41 per cent were having an income between Rs. 6000 and Rs. 8500. The percentage of the workers with incomes between Rs. 8500 and Rs. 11000, 18.37 and it was 12.24 for those having incomes of more than Rs. 11000. During 1991-92, the workers in the income group below Rs. 4000 were about 51 per cent less than in the previous year. The number of workers in the income group of Rs. 4000-Rs. 6000 was 42 per cent less than in the previous year, while that of the workers in the Rs. 6000 - Rs. 8500 income group was about 66 per cent higher than in the previous year. The number of workers in the income group of Rs. 8500 - Rs.11000 during this year was almost the same as in the preceding year while that of the workers with incomes of more than Rs. 11000.00 was about 63 per cent higher. During 1992-93, none of the workers in the Block was in the below Rs. 4000.00 income group while the number of those in the income group of Rs. 4000-Rs. 6000 was about 62 per cent less than in the previous year. The number of workers in the income group of Rs. 6000 - Rs. 8500.00 was also lower by about 61 per cent from that in the preceding year while that of the workers in the Rs. 11000.00 and above group was 57 per cent higher. A comparison of the income profile of the beneficiaries of the two the Blocks reveals the following:

(i) The number of workers having income below Rs. 4000 was less in the R.M.Block than in the M.B. Block

(ii) The number of workers having income of more than Rs. 11000 was more in the M.B. than in the R.M. Block.

Per Capita Expenditure of the Beneficiaries

Table 6.8: Per Capita Yearly Expenditure of Beneficiaries Average Expenditure alongwith Household sizes

Beneficiaries Classifications	*M.B. Group*		*R.M. Block*	
	Average Expenditure (Rs.)	*Average Household Size*	*Average Expenditure (Rs.)*	*Average Household Size*
SC	1872.93	4.35	1827.88	4.86
Other	2237.63	4.81	2341.73	4.92
Women	2026.00	4.35	—	—
Landless	1981.15	4.34	2103.00	4.05

Table 6.8 shows the per capita expenditure and the average sizes of the households of the sampled beneficiary.

In the M.B. Block, the average per capita expenditure was Rs. 1872.93 in the case of the SCs, Rs. 2237.63 in the case of others and Rs. 1981.15 in that of the landless workers. The per capita expenditure in the households where women worked under JRY was Rs. 2026.00. It means the SCs have the lowest per capita expenditure and 'others' have the highest in between the two is the per capita expenditure of the landless workers. It is interesting to note that the per capita expenditure of the households of women beneficiaries is more than that of the

SCs the and the landless categories of the workers. It points to the women contribution in raising the expenditure level of the households.

In the R.M. Block, the per capita expenditure of the households of the SC beneficiaries was Rs. 1827.88. It was Rs. 2341.73 in the case of the 'others' and Rs. 2103.00 in that of the landless worker households as the table shows. In this Block the per capita expenditure of the SC category was the lowest and that of the others was the highest with the per capita expenditure of the landless workers occupying the middle position.

Comparing the figures for the two Blocks, we find that in both the Blocks the SCs have the lowest per capita expenditure and 'others' have the highest. The disparity between the per capita expenditure of the SCs and that of the 'other' categories of the workers is also higher in the R.M. Block than in the M.B. Block, the gap being about 28 per cent in the former and about 19 per cent in the latter. Besides, the disparity between the per capita expenditure levels of the SCs and the landless workers is also more in the R.M. Block than in the M.B. Block. It is about 15 per cent in the former and about 6 per cent in the latter. In a nut shell, the R.M. Block is better placed in this respect than the M.B. Block.

Beneficiaries under Other Anti Poverty Programmes:

Table 6.9 presents the details of sampled households benefiting from other anti-poverty programmes such as IRDP, in the two Blocks.

In the M.B. Block, 57.72 per cent of the total number of the beneficiaries have got assistance under other anti poverty programmes. In the case of the SCs 64.15 per cent were benefited from these programmes while of those in the category of 'others' 41.86 benefited from them. The percentages for the landless workers and the women were 55.41 and 88.89 respectively. Overall the SCs accounted for the maximum number of the beneficiaries assisted under the other anti poverty programmes.

In the R.M. Block, 38.67 per cent of the beneficiaries had benefited from the other anti poverty programmes. In the

Table 6.9: Details of Beneficiaries assisted under other Anti Poverty Programmes

Classification of Beneficiaries	*M.B. Block*			*R. M. Block*		
	Benefitted	*Not Benefitted*	*Total*	*Benefitted*	*Not Benefitted*	*Total*
Total	86	63	149	58	92	150
	(57.72)	(42.28)	(100.00)	(38.67)	61.33)	(100.00)
SC	68	38	106	50	53	103
	(64.15)	35.85)	(100.00)	(48.54)	(51.46)	(100.00)
Other	18	25	43	8	39	47
	(41.86)	58.14)	(100.00)	(17.02)	(82.98)	(100.00)
Women	8	1	9	—	—	—
	(88.89)	(11.11)	(100.00)			
Landless Labour	41	33	74	40	71	111
	(55.41)	(44.59)	(100.00)	(36.04)	(63.96)	(100.00)

Figures in Parentheses show the percentages.

Table 6.10 : Details of the belonging areas of Beneficiaries

Classification of the Beneficiaries	*M.B. Block*					*R.M. Block*				
	Same Village	*Same Block*	*Same Dist.*	*Same State*	*Other State*	*Same Village*	*Same Block*	*Same Dist.*	*Same State*	*Other State*
SC	105	1	—	—	—	98	—	—	—	—
Other	43	—	—	—	—	40	12	—	—	—
Women	9	—	—	—	—	—	—	—	—	—
Landless	—	—	—	—	—	—	—	—	—	—

case of the SCs this percentage was 48.54 and in that of 'others' it was 17.02. The landless workers 36.04 per cent fell in this category. In this block the SC topped the list of the beneficiaries receiving assistence under the antipoverty programmes.

Table 6.10 shows the belonging areas of the beneficiaries in both the Blocks. In the M.B. Block all the workers except one belonged to the same village. This worker belonged to an other village but in the same Block. In the R.M. Blocks, 139 or 92 per cent of the total workers belonged to the same village and the rest 12 (8%) belonged to other villages but in the same Block. This shows that in the R.M. Block the employment benefits of the JRY had not gone entirely to the village for which the funds under the scheme had been allocated.

Summing up

To conclude, about 70 per cent of the total beneficiaries belonged to the SC category and about 75 per cent of the total in both the Blocks were landless. Women accounted for only 6 per cent of the beneficiaries that too only in the MB Block. In this Block about 47 per cent of the beneficiaries were landless workers, about 95 per cent were marginal farmers, about 6 per cent were small farmers and about 3 per cent were artisans while in the R.M. Block about 75 per cent were landless, 25 per cent were marginal farmers and none was from small farmer and artisans categories. The pattern of the wage earners is found to be almost the same in both the Blocks. Most of the households in both the Blocks were having only one wage earner. In the M.B. Block, about 72 per cent workers had kachha houses while in the RM Block the workers in this category were about 68 per cent of the total. Among the workers, illiteracy was found to be more in the R.M. than in the M.B. Block. In terms of the capita expenditure, workers of the R.M. Block were better placed than those of the M.B. Block. About 56 per cent of the workers in the M.B. Block had benefitted from other anti-poverty programmes while about 31 per cent of them in the RM Block had received this benefit. In the M.B. Block, almost all the workers belonged to the same village while in the R.M. Block 8 per cent of them did not belong to the same village but belonged to the same Block.

7

CAPITAL FORMATION UNDER THE JRY

Introduction

In this chapter the assets created under the JRY in both the Blocks during the reference period (1990-91 to 1992-93) are discussed. The discussion is centered around the number of the assets created, actual expenditure incurred on them, the ratio of the total expenditure to individual assets, wage and non - wage ratios, average expenditure per asset as well as per panchayat, quality of the assets created, their impact on the life of the people and their maintenance.

Creation of Assets during 1990-91

Table 7.1 shows the numbers and types of assets created during 1990-91 in the two Blocks. As the table shows in the MB Block kachha road (earth work), khadanja (vertical brick laying) padanja (horizontal brick laying) and culverts were built during the year. These assets numbering thirty five, 4.29 per cent (12) were kachha road, 57.14 per cent (20) were khadanja, 5.70 per cent (2) were padanja and 2.86(1) were culverts. If we look at the expenditure on creation of the various assets we find a similar pattern because of the total expenditure incurred, 77.30 per cent was on the construction of khadanja and 16.57 per cent on that of kachha road. If we combine the expenditure on these two items find that they had accounted for as much as about 95 per cent of the total allocation. It shows the necessity for construction of both kachha roads and khadanjas in the villages in the Block during the year.

Table 7.1: Types of Assets created during 1990-91

Sl. No.	*Name of Assets*	*No. of Asset Created*	*Actual Expenditure (Rs.)*	*Expenditure on wages (Rs.)*	*Expenditure on material (Rs.)*	*Wage and non-wage Ratio*	*Average Expenditure per Panchayat (Rs.)*	*Average Expenditure per asset (Rs.)*
1	*2*	*3*	*4*	*5*	*6*	*7*	*8*	*9*
	M.B. Block							
1.	Kachha Road	12 (34.29)	65749.43 (16.57)	65749.43	—	100 :00	10958.24	5479.12
2.	Khadanja	20 (57.14)	306702.35 (77.30)	98144.75	208557.59	32:68	51117.06	15335.12
3.	Padanja	2 (5.70)	22643.73 (5.71)	5660.93	16982.80	25:75	3773.96	11321.87
4.	School/Panchayat Building	—	—	—	—	—	—	—
5.	Land Development	—	—	—	—	—	—	—
6.	Flood/Water Control	—	—	—	—	—	—	—
7.	Village Tank/Well	—	—	—	—	—	—	—
8.	Culvert	1 (2.86)	1652.36 (0.42)	793.13	859.23	48:52	275.39	1652.36
9.	Others	—	—	—	—	—	—	—
10.	Total	35 (100.00)	396748.00 (100.00)	170601.64	226146.36	43:57	66124.67	11335.66

[contd..]

Table 7.1 [contd.]

Sl. No.	Name of Assets	No. of Asset Created	Actual Expenditure (Rs.)	Expenditure on wages (Rs.)	Expenditure on material (Rs.)	Wage and non-wage Ratio	Average Expenditure per Panchayat (Rs.)	Average Expenditure per asset (Rs.)
1	2	3	4	5	6	7	8	9
	R.M. Block							
1.	Kachha Road	6 (24.00)	63678.70 (21.83)	61131.55	2547.15	96:04	12735.74	10613.12
2.	Khadanja	9 (36.00)	136001.94 (46.62)	81601.16	54400.78	60:40	27200.39	15111.33
3.	Padanja	6 (24.00)	62082.45 (21.28)	11795.67	50286.78	19:81	12416.45	10347.08
4.	School/Panchayat Building	1 (4.00)	11151.46 (3.82)	3010.89	8140.57	27:73	2230.29	11151.46
5.	Land Development	—	—	—	—	—	—	—
6.	Flood/Water Control	—	—	—	—	—	—	—
7.	Village Tank/Well	—	—	—	—	—	—	—
8.	Culvert	—	—	—	—	—	—	—
9.	Others	3 (12.20)	18818.45 (6.45)	5645.54	13172.91	30:70	3763.69	6272.82
10.	Total	25 (100.00)	291733.00 (100.00)	166287.81	125445.19	57:43	58346.60	11669.32

Columns 5 and 6 show the wage and non-wage expenditure on creation of the assets during the reference year. At the Block level the ratio between the two was 43:57 it differed from asset to asset. For example, in the first case of kachha roads it was 100:00 which means that the total funds were spent on wages only. In case of khadanja, however this ratio is 32:68. It is 25:75 in the case of padanja and is 48:52 in that of culvert. As per JRY guidelines (1991), at least 60 per cent of the total allocation should be spent on wages. Except in the construction of Kachha roads, where only wage expenditure was incurred in the creation of asset has the wage and non-wage ratio been no other in accordance with the guidelines of the JRY. Actually, prescription of such ratios is not a practicable proposition. During the course of our investigation we found that all officials and non officials from the Gram Sabha to the DRDA were against fixing of this minimum limit. They suggested that the decision in this regard should be left to the implementing agency which would decide the ratio according to the type and nature of the asset. The average expenditure per panchayat at the Block level was Rs.66124.67 which varied from asset to asset as the table shows. The average expenditure per panchayat for Kachha road, Khadanja, Padanja and culvert was Rs. 10958.24 Rs. 51117.06 Rs. 3773.96 and Rs. 275.39 respectively. The average expenditure per asset at the Block level was Rs. 11335.66. This varied from asset to asset as was Rs. 5479.12 for Kachha road Rs. 15335.12 for Khadanja and Rs. 11321.87 for Padanja.

In the R.M. Block, the pattern of assets creation was almost the same as in the other Block in the sense that the expenditure on the kachha roads, Khadanja and Padanjas accounted for the bulk of the total expenditure. The same was true of the number of the assets created of which 36 per cent were Khadanjas, 24 per cent kachha roads and an equal percentage padanjas. Of the total expenditure, 46.62 per cent, 21.83 per cent, 21.28 per cent went to khadanjas, kachha roads and padanjas, respectively. If we club these three assets together, we find that they had accounted for as much as about 90 per cent of the total expenditure. But if we compare the pattern in this Block with that in M.B. Block, we find that in the latter Block comparatively more money was allocated to these three items together as the table shows. It means in the MB Block necessity for construction of streets was more acute than in the M.B. Block.

Wage and non-wage ratio at the Block level in the RM

Block was 57:43. However, it varied from asset to asset. For example it was 96:04 in the case of kachha roads, 19:81 in the case of padanjas and 60:40 in that of khadanjas. The wage and non-wage ratio both in aggregate and individual asset levels was better in this Block in the sense that it was less wide off the JRY norm of 60:40. In other words in this Block more resources were invested in the creation of persondays than in the other Block.

The average expenditure per panchayat in the R.M. Block was Rs. 58346.60 which is about Rs.8000.00 less than that in the M.B. Block. The reason is obvious as this Block is more developed than the M.B. Block and hence got less allocation than the latter. Secondly here the ratio of the SC population to the total village population was also less than in the M.B. Block. These variables are the basic determinant in the allocation of resources under the JRY.

The average asset wise expenditure in the R.M. Block was Rs. 11669.32 which is almost equal to that in the M.B. Block.

Asset Creation during 1991-92

During 1991-92, of the total assets created in the M.B. Block, 34.78 per cent were kachha roads, 43.48 per cent Khadanjas and 13.04 per cent were padanjas. School/panchayat buildings and other assets were 4.35 per cent each. Of the total expenditure incurred, 13.19 per cent was on the construction of kachha roads, 68.88 per cent on the construction of khadanja, 10.55 per cent on the construction of school / panchayat buildings, 6.54 per cent on the construction of the padanjas and the rest the construction of the other assets. During this year the maximum amount of the expenditure under the JRY was on in the construction of khadanjas followed by that on the construction of kachha roads. It may be noted here that a diversification in the formation of assets has taken place as more types of assets were created during this year.

The wage and none - wage ratio in this Block during the year was 61:39 which showed a noticeable improvement from the previous year. However, the assetwise ratios varied from this overall ratio. For example, in the construction of kachha roads, it was 100:00. While in that of khadanjas it was 27:73. The average expenditure per asset was Rs. 10856.83. If we compare this level of per asset expenditure with the previous year's level we find that it is not much different. In the case

Table 7.2: Types of Assets created during 1991-92

Sl. No.	Name of Assets	No. of Asset Created	Actual Expenditure (Rs.)	Expenditure on wage (Rs.)	Expenditure on material (Rs.)	Wage and non-wage Ratio	Average Expenditure per Panchayat (Rs.)	Average Expenditure per asset (Rs.)
1	2	3	4	5	6	7	8	9
	M.B. Block							
1.	Kachha Road	8 (34.78)	32943.38 (13.19)	32943.38	—	100:00	5490.56	4119.92
2.	Khadanja	10 (43.48)	171992.13 (68.88)	46437.88	125554.25	27:73	2865.54	17199.21
3.	Padanja	3 (13.04)	16338.38 (6.54)	6535.35	9803.03	40:60	2723.06	5446.13
4.	School/Panchayat Building	1	26344.58 (10.55)	6322.70	200031.88	24:76	4390.76	26344.58
5.	land Development	—	—	—	—	—	—	—
6.	Flood/Water Control	—	—	—	—	—	—	—
7.	Village Tank/Well	—	—	—	—	—	—	—
8.	Culvert	—	—	—	—	—	—	—
9.	Others	1 (4.35)	2088.53 (0.84)	1274.00	814.53	61:39	348.09	2088.53
10.	Total	23 (100.00)	249707.00 (100.00)	92391.59	157315.41	37:63	41617.83	10856.83

[contd..]

Table 7.2 [contd.]

Sl. No.	Name of Assets	No. of Asset Created	Actual Expenditure (Rs.)	Expenditure on wages (Rs.)	Expenditure on material (Rs.)	Wage and non-wage Ratio	Average Expenditure per Panchayat (Rs.)	Average Expenditure per asset (Rs.)
1	2	3	4	5	6	7	8	9
	R.M. Block							
1.	Kachha Road	10 (52.63)	101359.10 (46.99)	91223.19	10135.91	90:10	20271.82	10135.91
2.	Khadanja	5 (26.32)	56121.80 (26.02)	5050.96	51070.84	9:91	11224.36	11227.36
3.	Padanja	—	—	—	—	—	—	—
4.	School/Panchayat Building	2 (10.56)	44502.82 (20.64)	13795.87	30706.95	31:69	8900.56	22251.41
5.	Land Development	—	—	—	—	—	—	—
6.	Flood/Water Control	—	—	—	—	—	—	—
7.	Village Tank/Well	—	—	—	—	—	—	—
8.	Culvert	—	—	—	—	—	—	—
9.	Others	2 (10.56)	13700.85 (6.35)	5480.34	8220.51	40:60	2740.17	6850.43
10.	Total	19 (100.00)	215684.50 (100.00)	116469.63	99214.87	54:46	43136.90	11351.82

Figures in Parentheses show the percentages.

of the average expenditure per panchayat however the difference is wide. As against Rs. 66124.67 in the previous year the level of this expenditure in this year was only Rs. 41617.83, which is about 37 per cent lower. The reason for this reduction is that the total expenditure incurred during this year was also less than that of the previous year.

During 1991-92 out of the total assets created in the RM Block 52.63 per cent were kachha roads, 26.32 per cent khadanjas and 10.55 per cent each were school panchayat buildings and other assets. Similarly, of the total expenditure incurred, 46.99 per cent was on the construction of kachha roads, 26.2 per cent on the construction of khadanjas, 20.63 per cent on the construction of the school / panchayat buildings and the rest on the building of the other assets. It may be noticed that no padanja work had been carried out during the year. If we compare the assets built during this year in this Block with those built in the other Block we find that in its case kachha roads work has been given more importance. This is also true of this school/panchayat buildings. If we compare the assetwise expenditure in this year with that in the previous year, we find that the expenditure on kachha roads was more in this year than in the previous year. However, the expenditure on the construction of khadanjas also came down during this year. In the previous year the padanjas had got about 21 per cent of the total expenditure, during this year they got nothing as the table shows. But more money had been spent on the construction of school/panchayat buildings during this year than in the previous year. This shows that after road construction that of school buildings had received priority. Since this basic necessity at the grassroots levels it shows that the panchayats were well aware of their problems and priorities.

The wage and non-wage ratio at the Block level in the RM Block during the year was 54:46 which showed a deterioration from the previous year when it was 57:43. However, the assetwise ratios differed widely from this aggregate ratio. It was as low as 9:91 in the construction of khadanja and as high as 90:10 in that of kachha roads. However even in the construction of kachha roads in which soil is supposed to be used some non-wage expenditure has been shown. It is due to the reason that cement pipes had also been used in the construction of kachha roads for supplying water from one side to the other.

The average expenditure per panchayat in this Block in this year was Rs. 43136.90 which was lower than its level in the previous year but was more than that in the M.B. Block. The average expenditure per asset was Rs.11351.82 which is almost equal to that in the previous year and also nearly the same as its level in the M.B. Block in this year.

Creation of Asset during 1992-93

Table 7.3 depicts the pattern of the assets created in both thc Blocks. In the M.B. Block, of the total assets created, 52.94 per cent were khadanjas, 14.71 per cent padanjas, 5.88 per cent each were kachha roads and flood and water control and the rest were school/panchayat buildings. Similarly, of the total expenditure incurred about 64 per cent went to the construction of khadanjas, about 4 per cent to that of kachha roads about 11 per cent to the construction of culverts and the rest went to the construction of padanja, school/panchayat building and flood control activities. If we compare this pattern of construction of various assets during 1992-93 to that in the previous year, we find that the expenditure on kachha roads has been reduced obviously because during the last three years of the Scheme's operation, all the kachha roads required to be built had been built. Although the construction of khadanjas received the same priority in this year as it had in the earlier years also, the position of kachha roads and padanjas in the scale of preferences had been taken over by activities like conservation/preservation and development of water and soil resources. Besides, Priority had also been given to the construction of culverts and school/panchayat buildings.

The wage and non-wage ratio during this year was 38:62 as the table shows. There is not much difference between this ratio and those for the previous two years as it has remained around 40 throughout as against the JRY guideline of 60. But in respect of individual assets it has ranged from 100:00 in kachha roads to 25:75 for padanjas.

The average expenditure per panchayat in this year was Rs.77150.00 which is higher than in the earlier years. Similarly, the average expenditure per asset was more in this year than it was in the previous year.

In the R.M. Block of the total assets created, 43.48 were khadanjas, 21.74 per cent were kachha roads 13.04 per cent were padanjas and the rest were school/panchayats, land

Table 7.3 : Assets created during 1992-93

Sl. No.	*Name of Assets*	*No. of Asset Created*	*Actual Expenditure (Rs.)*	*Expenditure on wages (Rs.)*	*Expenditure on material (Rs.)*	*Wage and non-wage Ratio*	*Average Expenditure per Panchayat (Rs.)*	*Average Expenditure per asset (Rs.)*
1	*2*	*3*	*4*	*5*	*6*	*7*	*8*	*9*
	M.B. Block							
1.	Kachha Road	2 (5.88)	17704.20 (3.82)	17704.20	—	100 : 00	2950.70	8852.10
2.	Khadanja	18 (52.94)	295968.48 (63.94)	109508.33	186460.15	37:63	49328.08	16442.69
3.	Padanja	5 (14.71)	39796.23 (8.60)	9949.06	29847.17	25:75	6632.71	7959.25
4.	School/Panchayat Building	1 (2.94)	31255.54 (6.75)	8751.55	24379.32	28:78	5209.26	31255.54
5.	Land Development	—	—	—	—	—	—	—
6.	Flood/Water Control	2 (5.88)	15805.44 (3.41)	10747.70	5057.74	68:32	2634.24	7902.72
7.	Village Tank/Well	—	—	—	—	—	—	—
8.	Culvert	3 (8.82)	51858.58 (11.20)	13483.23	38375.35	26:74	8643.10	17286.19
9.	Others	3 (8.82)	10511.53 (2.27)	6937.61	3573.92	66:34	1751.92	3503.84
10.	Total	34 (100.00)	462900.00 (100.00)	175902.00	286998.00	38:62	77150.00	13614.71

[contd..]

Table 7.3 [contd.]

Sl. No.	Name of Assets	No. of Asset Created	Actual Expenditure (Rs.)	Expenditure on wages (Rs.)	Expenditure on material (Rs.)	Wage and non-wage Ratio	Average Expenditure per Panchayat (Rs.)	Average Expenditure per asset (Rs.)
1	2	3	4	5	6	7	8	9
	R.M. Block							
1.	Kachha Road	5 (21.74)	61267.89 (18.37)	61267.89	—	100:00	12253.58	12253.58
2.	Khadanja	10 (43.48)	179291.31 (53.75)	39444.09	139847.22	22:78	35858.26	17929.13
3.	Padanja	3 (13.04)	28100.31 (8.42)	2810.03	25290.28	10:90	5620.56	9366.77
4.	School/Panchayat Building	2 (8.70)	14547.41 (4.36)	5818.96	8728.45	40:60	2909.48	7273.71
5.	Land Development	1 (4.35)	24394.54 (7.31)	12197.27	12197.27	50:50	4878.91	24394.54
6.	Flood/Water Control	—	—	—	—	—	—	—
7.	Village Tank/Well	—	—	—	—	—	—	—
8.	Culvert	1 (4.35)	17819.59 (5.34)	5167.68	12651.91	29:71	3563.92	17819.59
9.	Others	1 (4.35)	8167.96 (2.45)	1633.59	6534.37	20:80	8167.96	1633.59
10.	Total	23 (100.00)	333589.00 (100.00)	126763.82	206825.18	38:62	66717.80	14503.87

development, flood/water control and culverts. Similarly, of the total expenditure incurred, more than 70 per cent was spent on the construction of kachha roads and khadanjas and the rest 30 per cent was spent on the creation of the other assets. As compared to previous year, the share of the construction of kachha roads in this year was lower whereas that of the construction of khadanjas was higher. In this year the development of land activity was also taken up. The wage and non wage ratio was 38:62 as the table shows. This is lower than in the previous year.

The average expenditure per panchayat was Rs. 66717.80 during 1992-93 which was more than its level in previous year's. The average expenditure per asset was Rs.14503.87 which had been remained almost the same during the three years reference period.

It may be noted that in this particular year both the Blocks had witnessed some diversification in the creation of assets.

The following conclusions may be drawn from the above discussion.

(i) Constructions of Khadanjas, Padanjas and Kachha roads have been the dominent activities for creation of assets during the reference period. But their dominance has been decreasing even if slightly year after year.

(ii) Diversification of the activities relating to creation of the community assets has been taking place year after year, more particularly in the last year of the reference period. The trend has been towards activities like preservation and conservation of soil and water resources from those relating to building of community assets like roads, Khadanjas, etc.

(iii) The JRY guideline said that atleast 60 per cent of the resources should be spent of wages, has not been adhered to in the construction of assets.

(iv) The average expenditure per panchayat and the average expenditure per asset have not shown any particular trend as they depend on the allocations to the panchayats under the scheme and the number of assets created during the period.

Maintenance of assets

Maintenance of assets is as important as is their creation. Table 7.4 shows the expenditure incurred on the maintenance of the different types of assets created during the reference years. Before discussing the issue it may be mentioned that as per the JRY guidelines a maximum of 10 per cent of the total expenditure could be incurred on this item.

In 1990-91, of the total expenditure incurred on the creation of various assets in the MB Block 7.88 per cent had been spent on maintenance of the assets. Assetwise, it was 9.29 per cent of the total in the case of kachha road and, 7.41 per cent in that of khadanjas. The shares of padanjas and culverts were

Table 7.4 : Maintenance of assets created under the JRY

Sl. No.	*Name of Assets*	*1990-91*	*1991-92*	*1992-93*
		Percentage of mainte-nance expenditure to total expenditure	*Percentage of mainte-nance expenditure to total expenditure*	*Percentage of mainte-nance expenditure to total expenditure*
1	*2*	*3*	*4*	*5*
M.B. Block				
1.	Kachha Road	9.29	16.97	11.47
2.	Khadanja	7.41	10.86	8.56
3.	Padanja	10.16	5.51	1.83
4.	School/Panchayat Building	—	8.43	6.24
5.	Land Development	—	—	—
6.	Flood/Water Control	—	—	0.63
7.	Village Tank/Well	—	—	—
8.	Culvert	9.08	—	7.81
9.	Other	—	—	11.42
10.	Total	7.88	10.42	7.65
R.M. Block				
1.	Kachha Road	12.53	12.75	11.87
2.	Khadanja	13.11	9.27	10.24
3.	Padanja	7.25	—	18.80
4.	School/ Panchayat Building	9.15	1.35	1.37
5.	Land Development	—	—	1.89
6.	Flood/Water Control	—	—	—
7.	Village Tank/ Well	—	—	—
8.	Culvert	—	—	12.35
9.	Other	—	3.89	25.27
10.	Total	11.80	8.93	10.74

10.16 per cent and 9.08 per cent respectively. During 1991-92, of the total expenditure in this Block 10.42 per cent was on the maintenance of assets. Assetwise it ranged from 16.97 per cent in the case of Kachha road to 5.51 per cent in that of padanjas. In this year the percentage of the expenditure on this item was about 32 per cent higher than in the previous year. This shows the growing consciousness among the people about maintenance of the assets. During 1992-93, of the total expenditure, only about 8 per cent had been spent on maintenance of the assets. Thus, it had been reduced from previous year's level by almost as much as it had been increased during 1991-92 from the level in the base year 1990-91. Assetwise expenditure on this particular item during 1992-93 ranged from 11.47 per cent in the case of kachha roads to 0.63 in that case of flood/water control. Overall, the expenditure on maintenance of assets, in this Block does not show any particular pattern.

Let us examine the maintenance of assets in the RM Block. Here, in 1990-91, of the total expenditure on this item 11.80 per cent had been spent on the maintenance of assets. Assetwise it was 12.53 per cent in the case of kachha roads, 13.90 per cent in that of khadanjas, 7.25 per cent on padanjas and 9.15 per cent on school/panchayat buildings. In the case of the other assets created, no amount was spent on their maintenance. During 1991-92 the overall percentage at 8.93 was lower than the 1990-91 level of 11.80. Assetwise the maintenance expenses were 12.75 per cent kachha roads, 9.27 on khadanjas, 1.35 per cent on school/panchayat buildings and 3.89 on other types of assets. Comparison of these percentages with those for the previous year shows that except for kachha roads the maintenance ratios had decreased. The maximum reduction was in the case of school/panchayat buildings.

During 1992-93 the expenditure on maintenance of assets constructed 10.74 per cent of the total which is more than its share in the previous year but lower than the 1990-91 level. The assetwise distribution of the expenses on maintenance is markedly skewed because it ranges from 1.37 per cent in the case of school building to 25.22 per cent in that of the other assets. From the above discussion the following conclusions emerge:

(i) The ratios of the expenditure on the maintenance of the assets to the total expenditure during the reference period in both the Blocks indicate by and large no norms have been adopted. The level has been determined by the needs of the situation.

(ii) Judging from the maintenance ratios in the two Blocks it can be said that the assets in the R.M Block have been better maintained than those in the MB Block.

(iii) More expenditure on maintenance of assets has been incurred on kachha roads khadanjas and padanjas and assets in the categories of others than on that of buildings such as school and panchayats and conservation of soil and water resources which in fact has been meager.

Quality of the Assets Created

Table 7.5 gives a picture of the quality of the assets created in the sampled panchayats of the two Blocks. The quality has been graded as excellent, very good, good/ satisfactory, poor and not usable. Its measurement is based on the responses of the beneficiaries and the judgment of the investigator.

Let us first discuss the position in the MB Block. During 1990-91, 75 per cent of the total created in this Block were found to be very good and the rest 25 per cent either good or satisfactory. An assetwise analysis showed that of the total kachha roads, 68.75 per cent were very good and 31.25 per cent were either good or satisfactory. In the case of khadanjas 76 per cent of the total were found to be in very good condition and 24 per cent in good/satisfactory condition. All padanjas and culverts constructed during the year were found to be very good. None of the assets created was found to be excellent, poor and not usable.

During 1991-92, the quality of the assets created had deteriorated because only 57.89 per cent of them were found to be of very good quality and the rest were either good or satisfactory. Assetwise of the total Kachha road constructed, 33.33 per cent were found to be very good and 66.67 per cent either good or satisfactory. In the case of the Khadanjas while the percentage of those at very good quality went down from 76 to 66.76 that of assets of good or satisfactory quality went up from 24 to 33.33. Of the total Padanjas created about 83 per cent were found to be of very good quality and the rest

Table 7.5: Quality of Assets Created

S. No.	Name of Assets	1990-91 Quality of Assets					1991-92 Quality of Assets					1992-93 Quality of Assets				
		E	VG	G/S	P	N.U	E	VG	G/S	P	N.U	E	VG	G/S	P	N.U
1	2	3	4	5	6	7	8	9	10	11	12	13	14	15	16	17
	M.B. Block															
1.	Kachha Road	—	68.75	31.25	—	—	—	33.33	66.67	—	—	—	100.00	—	—	—
2.	Khadanja	—	76.00	24.00	—	—	—	66.76	33.33	—	—	—	59.89	40.91	—	—
3.	Padanja	—	100.00	—	—	—	—	83.33	16.67	—	—	—	60.00	40.00	—	—
4.	Land Development	—	—	—	—	—	—	100.00	—	—	—	—	—	—	—	—
5.	Flood/Panchayat Building	—	—	—	—	—	—	—	—	—	—	—	100.00	—	—	—
6.	School/Panchayat Building	—	—	—	—	—	—	—	—	—	—	—	—	—	—	—
7.	Village Tank/Well	—	—	—	—	—	—	—	—	—	—	—	—	—	—	—
8.	Culvert	—	100.00	—	—	—	—	—	—	—	—	—	—	—	—	—
9.	Others	—	—	—	—	—	—	—	—	—	—	—	—	—	—	—
10.	Total/Average	—	75.00	25.00	—	—	—	57.89	42.11	—	—	—	63.16	36.84	—	—

[contd..]

Table 7.5 (contd.)

S. No.	Name of Assets	*1990-91* Quality of Assets					*1991-92* Quality of Assets					*1992-93* Quality of Assets				
		E	VG	G/S	P	N.U	E	VG	G/S	P	N.U	E	VG	G/S	P	N.U
1	2	3	4	5	6	7	8	9	10	11	12	13	14	15	16	17
M.B. Block																
1.	Kachha Road	—	83.33	16.67	—	—	—	69.23	30.77	—	—	—	83.33	16.67	—	—
2.	Khadanja	—	90.94	9.09	—	—	—	40.00	60.00	—	—	—	70.00	30.00	—	—
3.	Padanja	—	33.33	66.67	—	—	—	—	—	—	—	—	66.67	33.33	—	—
4.	School/Panchayat Building	—	—	100.00	—	—	—	50.00	50.00	—	—	—	100.00	—	—	—
5.	Land Development	—	—	—	—	—	—	—	—	—	—	—	—	—	—	—
6.	Flood/Water Control	—	—	—	—	—	—	—	—	—	—	—	—	—	—	—
7.	Village Tank/Well	—	—	—	—	—	—	—	—	—	—	—	—	—	—	—
8.	Culvert	—	—	—	—	—	—	100.00	—	—	—	—	—	—	—	—
9.	Others	—	66.67	33.33	—	—	—	100.00	—	—	—	—	100.00	—	—	—
10.	Total/Average	—	70.37	29.63	—	—	—	63.64	36.36	—	—	—	78.26	21.74	—	—

Note : E=Excellent, VG=Very Good, G/S=Good/Satisfactory, P=Poor, NU=Not Usable.

of good/satisfactory quality. Land development was found to be 100 per cent of in very good quality.

During 1992-93, the analysis of the data shows that at the Block level of the total assets created 63.16 per cent were of very good quality and 36.84 per cent were of good/satisfactory quality. It shows that the quality of the created assets improved from the 1991-92 level but it was still worse than the quality of the assets created during 1990-91. The assetwise analysis for this year shows that all the kachha roads were of very good quality as against only about 33 per cent in the previous year. The quality status of both khadanjas and padanjas had come down from the 1991-92 level as table shows. The quality of all the flood/water control works and school/panchayat buildings was also found to be very good.

In the R.M. Block, during 1990-91, 70.37 per cent, of the total assets created were found to be of very good quality and the rest were of either good or satisfactory quality. An assetwise analysis shows that of the total kachha roads, 83.33 per cent were of very good quality and 16.67 were of good/satisfactory quality. In the cases Khadanjas as many as more than 90 per cent were found in very good condition. However, only 33.33 per cent of Padanjas were found in this condition and the remaining 66.67 per cent were found to be of a good/satisfactory quality. All the school/panchayat buildings were found to be either of good or satisfactory quality while 66.67 per cent of the other assets were found in a very good condition. During 1991-92, 63.64 per cent of the total assets were found to be of very good quality and 36.36 per cent of good/satisfactory quality. Like the MB Block in this Block also the quality of the assets created deteriorated during the year. But the degree of deterioration in its case was less than it was in the M.B Block as it was about 10 per cent as against about 22 per cent in the latter. An assetwise analysis shows that 69.23 per cent of kachha roads were found to be of a very good quality and 40 per cent of khadanjas also were found to be of the same quality. Half of the school/panchayat buildings also fell in the same categories while their other half of them were of good quality. Hundred per cent of other types of assets also belonged to the very good quality.

During 1992-93, 78.26 per cent of the assets created were found to be of a very good quality and the rest were of a good/satisfactory quality. There was a remarkable improvement in the quality of the assets created during this year as compared to the earlier years. An assetwise analysis shows that 83.33 per cent of Kachha roads were of very good quality and 70 per cent of khadanjas and 66.67 of padanjas also fell in the same category. The rest of the assets such as school/panchayat buildings, culvert and other assets were found to be 100 per cent of very good quality.

The comparative picture, which emerges from this analysis shows that during 1991-92 the quality of the assets in both the Blocks had deteriorated from its level in earlier year. But the deterioration was severer in the M.B. Block than in the R.M. Block. During 1992-93, the level of the quality in both the Block improved but the improvement was more noticeable in the R.M. Block than in the M.B. Block. Overall, over the three year period as a whole, quality of the assets had been better in the R.M. Block than it was in the M.B. Block. One reason for this comparatively worse position of the BM Block could be its topography and soil conditions.

Except during 1990-91 and 1991-92, the quality of padanjas in the MB Block was not found to be very good. This was due to the nature of their construction because it is less sustainable than Khadanjas for in their case bricks are laid horizontally while in that of the latter, they are laid vertically.

Impact of Assets Creation on Village Life

One question put to the beneficiaries of the various assets created under the JRY during the three years in the two Blocks was whether their creation of these assets had improved the quality of their life. The reply sought was categories as (a) improved (b) partially improved and (c) no improvement. The answers given have been put assetwise in table 7.6. It shows that all the assets created under the scheme during the reference period have improved the quality of life in the villages. This improvement has two dimensions: (a) completely improved (b) partially improved. Let us see the position on these two counts in the different years in the two Blocks. In the MB Block, during 1990-91, 61.36 per cent of the assets completely improved the quality of life and the rest improved it partially. During 1991-92, 92.97 per cent of the assets have completely improved the quality of life showing a 19 per cent increase in this year from the previous one.

During 1992-93, as many as more than 89 per cent of the

Table 7.6: Impact of Asset Creation on Village Life

S. No.	Name of Assets	1990-91			1991-92			1992-93		
		Improved	*Partially Improved*	*No. Improvement*	*Improved*	*Partially Improved*	*No. Improvement*	*Improved*	*Partially Improved*	*No. Improvement*
1	*2*	*3*	*4*	*5*	*6*	*7*	*8*	*9*	*10*	*11*
	M.B. Block									
1.	Kachha Road	62.50	37.50	—	60.00	40.00	—	100.00	—	—
2.	Khadanja	60.00	40.00	—	78.57	21.43	—	81.82	18.18	—
3.	Padanja	50.00	50.00	—	83.33	16.67	—	100.00	—	—
4.	School/Panchayat Building	—	—	—	100.00	—	—	100.00	—	—
5.	Land Development	—	—	—	—	—	—	—	—	—
6.	Flood/Water Control	—	—	—	—	—	—	100.00	—	—
7.	Village Tank/Well	—	—	—	—	—	—	—	—	—
8.	Culvert	100.00	—	—	100.00	—	—	100.00	—	—
9.	Others	—	—	—	—	—	—	—	—	—
10.	Total	61.36	38.64	—	72.97	27.63	—	89.19	10.81	—

[contd..]

Table 7.6 (contd.)

S. No.	Name of Assets	1990-91			1991-92			1992-93		
		Improved	*Partially Improved*	*No. Improvement*	*Improved*	*Partially Improved*	*No. Improvement*	*Improved*	*Partially Improved*	*No. Improvement*
1	*2*	*3*	*4*	*5*	*6*	*7*	*8*	*9*	*10*	*11*
	R.M. Block									
1.	Kachha Road	66.67	33.33	—	76.97	23.03	—	83.33	16.67	—
2.	Khadanja	63.64	36.36	—	40.00	60.00	—	70.00	30.00	—
3.	School/Panchayat Building	100.00	—	—	100.00	—	—	100.00	—	—
4.	Land Development	—	—	—	—	—	—	—	—	—
5.	Flood/Water Control	—	—	—	—	—	—	—	—	—
6.	Padanja	83.33	16.67	—	—	—	—	66.69	33.33	—
7.	Village Tank/Well	—	—	—	—	—	—	—	—	—
8.	Culvert	—	—	—	—	—	—	100.00	—	—
9.	Others	100.00	—	—	100.00	—	—	100.00	—	—
10.	Total	74.07	25.93	—	72.73	27.27	—	80.00	20.00	—

assets improved the quality of life completely which shows an improvement of about 22 per cent over the previous year.

In the case of the R.M. Block, during 1990-91, 74.07 per cent of the assets improved the quality of life completely while 25.93 per cent improved it partially. During 1991-92, the first percentage has come down but only to a negligible extent. In other words, the status of improvement of life during this year remained almost the same as it was in the previous year. However, during 1992-93, 80 per cent of the assets improved the quality of life and 20 per cent improved partially.

Summing Up

To conclude, Kachha roads, khadanjas and padanjas were the major assets created during the reference period in the two Blocks. It means that due to lack of resources with the panchayats, village streets were in a bad condition. Except the some cases the prescribed wage ratio was not observed. The norms prescribed for the maintenance of assets exception have also not been generally followed in the sampled GPs during the reference period. All the assets created during the reference period have been either every good quality or of good/satisfactory quality. The assets created have improved the life of the villagers.

8

IMPACT OF THE YOJANA ON EMPLOYMENT GENERATION

Introduction

In this chapter, assetwise employment generation and beneficiarywise employment opportunities created, average incremental employment, opportunity cost of employment generation under the scheme, reasons for sacrificing other employment and distance of the work site from the workers' residence have been discussed.

Employment Generation at Panchayat Levels

Table 8.1 presents the employment generation at the Panchayat level from 1990-91 to 1992-93 in both the Blocks.

Let us take the M.B. Block first. In it the average amount spent per GP during the reference period has been given as item 3 in Table 8.1. It was Rs. 66124.67 during 1990-91, Rs. 41617.83 during 1991-92 and Rs. 77150.00 during 1992-93. It was the lowest during 1991-92 and the highest during 1992-93. The total persondays generated during 1990-91, 1991-92 and 1992-93 were 7384.00, 4111.00 and 7449.00 respectively. The pattern of employment generation therefore is also the same as that of the average amount spent during the reference period. Looking at the yearwise employment position of the beneficiaries we find that during 1990-91, the proportion of the persondays of employment of the SC beneficiaries to the total persondays of employment generated was 71.44 per cent.

Table 8.1 : Employment Generated at Panchayat Level

S.No.	Particulars	M.B. Block			R.M. Block		
		1990-91	*91-92*	*92-93*	*1990-91*	*91-92*	*92-93*
1.	No. of Gram Panchayats	6	6	6	5	5	5
2.	Amount utilized (Rs.)	396748.00	249707.00	462900.00	291733.00	215684.50	333589.00
3.	Average Amount per GP (Rs.)	66124.67	41617.83	77150.00	58346.60	43136.90	66717.80
4.	Total persondays generated (No.)	7384.00	4111.00	7449.00	5846.00	5254.00	5185.00
	(i) SC	5275.00	2792.00	5664.00	4617.00	4051.00	4056.00
		(71.44)	(67.92)	(76.04)	(78.98)	(77.10)	(78.23)
	(ii) Others	2109.00	1319.00	1785.00	1229.00	1213.00	1129.00
		(28.56)	(32.08)	(23.96)	(19.31)	(22.90)	(21.77)
	(iii) Women	238.00	255.00	648.00	—	—	—
		(3.22)	(6.20)	(8.70)	—	—	—
	(iv) Landless labourers	6078.00	3158.00	5694.00	4830.00	3996.00	4531.00
		(82.31)	(76.82)	(76.44)	(82.62)	(76.06)	(87.38)

[contd..]

Table 8.1(contd.)

S.No.	*Particulars*	*M.B. Block*			*R.M. Block*		
		1990-91	*91-92*	*92-93*	*1990-91*	*91-92*	*92-93*
5.	Average No. of Persondays generated per GP	1231.00	685.00	1242.00	1169.00	1051.00	1037.00
6.	Cost of employment generated per person (Rs.)	53.73	60.74	62.14	49.90	41.05	64.34
7.	Estimated no. of person could be fully employed assuming 300 days as full employment norm.						
	Total	24.61	13.70	24.83	19.49	17.51	17.28
	(i) SC	17.58	9.31	18.88	15.39	13.50	13.52
	(ii) Others	7.03	4.39	5.95	4.10	4.04	3.76
	(iii) Women	0.79	0.85	2.16	—	—	—
	(iv) Landless	2.26	10.53	18.98	16.10	13.32	15.10

Expenditure utilized for construction of Houses for weaker section is not included.
Figures in parentheses show the percentages.

It was 28.56 per cent for the others. The share of women was a meagre 3.22 and that of land less labourers 82.31 per cent. As per the JRY guidelines, the women share in the total persondays generated should be at least 30 per cent while in this Block it merely one tenth of the stipulated target. The average number of persondays generated per panchayat during this year was 1231.00. The cost involved in generation of one personday was Rs. 53.73. An attempt has also been made to estimate the number of the persons who could get employment under the scheme if full employment is assumed to be available for 300 days in a year. A number of researchers such as Pandey (1975), Mehra (1960), Ratnawat (1975) and Masum (1983) have accepted this as the norm for their studies. Cho (1961) in South Korea had assumed even 280 persondays as a level of full employment. Basing our study on the norm of 300 persondays, we find that during 1990-91 the persons fully employed in the 6 sampled in the Block under the scheme numbered 24.61 panchayats. Of them, 17.58 were from the SC category and 7.03 from others. Not even a single women full employment during the year whereas the number of the landless workers who got employment was 20.26.

During 1991-92, of the total persondays generated, 67.92 per cent went to the SCs and the rest to the others. The share of women was 6.20 per cent which was almost double of that in the previous year.

The share of the landless in the total employment generated during this year was about 77 per cent which was about 7 per cent less than in the previous year. During this year, the cost per personday generated worked out at Rs. 60.74 which was about 2 per cent higher than in the previous year. Assuming that 300 persondays constituted full employment about 14 person had been fully employed during the year. Of these, 9.31 were SCs and the rest were others. Of the total employed not even one was woman with the share of this category being a mere 0.85 per cent.

During 1992-93 the share of the SCs in the total persondays generated was 76.04 per cent which was about 12 per cent more than in the previous year but only about 5 per cent more than in 1990-91. The share of the others in the employment generated was lower by about 25 per cent from the previous year and 18 per cent less than the year before. During 1992-

93, the share of the women was 8.90 per cent which was about 40 per cent higher than the the preceding year. It may be noticed that the share of the women has been increasing from year to year. This is a welcome trend. The landless accounted for 76.44 per cent of the employment generated in this year. The cost of employment generation per person during the year worked out at Rs. 62.14 which was more than its level in the previous two years. On the basis of 300 day employment as the norms 24.83 persons were employed fully in the sampled GPs during the year. Of them 18.88 persons were SCs and 5.95 others, as the table shows. Women and the landless were 2.16 and 18.98 persons respectively.

Now let us discuss the employment situation in the R.M.Block. Here, of the total persondays generated during 1990-91 the SCs accounted for 78.98 per cent and the others the rest. No woman got employment not only during this year but also in the following two years of the reference period while according to the JRY guidelines, they should have got at least 30 per cent of the total employment generated under the scheme. The landless labourers accounted for more than 80 per cent of the employment generated during 1990-91. Average number of persondays generated per panchayat were 1169.00 during the year. The cost of generating employment per person worked out at Rs. 49.90. The number of persondays who could be employed fully assuming 300 days as the working period for full employment was 19.49.

During 1991-92, the share of SCs in the total persondays generated was 77.10 per cent which was about 2 per cent less than in the previous year while that of others was about 2 per cent higher than in the previous year. The share of the landless labourers was 76.06 per cent which was about 8 per cent lower than the 1990-91. The average number of persondays generated per panchayat during this year was 1051.00 which was about 10 per cent less than in the previous year. Assuming the full employment norm of 300 days the total number of the persons employed was 17.51 as the table shows.

During 1992-93, the share of the SCs in the total employment generated was 78.23 which was about 1 per cent higher than in the previous year but almost equal to that in the year before. The share of the others in the total employment generated was over 21.77 per cent which was almost equal to their share in the previous year and that of the landless workers was 87.38 per cent, 15 per cent higher than in the previous year. The average number of persondays generated per GP was 1037.00 which was 3 per cent less than their number in the previous year.

The cost per person employment generation worked out at Rs. 64.34 in 1992-93 which higher than in both the previous years. The estimated number of persons getting full employment assuming 300 persondays as the norm worked out at 17.28 which, almost the same as in the previous year.

Comparing the employment results under the scheme at the panchayat level during the reference period in the two Blocks we find:

(i) The share of the SCs in the total employment generated during the entire period was higher in the R.M. Block than in the M.B. Block. It was the lowest in the middle year of the reference period and the highest in its first year in both the Blocks.

(ii) While the share of the SCs in the total employment generated was higher in the R.M. Block during all the three years the position as regards the others was just the reverse as is natural since the total employment went only to there two categories.

(iii) The share of women in the total employment generated in the M.B. Block at 3.22, 6.20 and 8.90 per cent during 1990-91, 1991-92 and 1992-93 respectively was below the stipulated minimum of 30 per cent for JRY. But it is heartening to note that their share has been showing an upward trend on the other hand, in the R.M. Block, no women got employment under the scheme.

(iv) The share of landless in the total employment generated was around 80 per cent in both the Blocks. But in the M.B. Block their share has been decreasing year after year whereas in the other Block their trend is different. Here, while their share in the last of the three years showed an increase over that in the first year, in the middle year, it was lower than both.

(v) The average number of persondays generated per GP

was the highest in the first year and the lowest in the middle year in the M.B. Block. However, it increased in the next year and reached almost the same level as in the first year. In the R.M. Block, while it was the highest in the first year the lowest level was reached in the last year of the reference period.

(vi) The cost of employment generation per person was higher in the M.B. Block than in the R.M. Block. Actually, the average number of person days generated per Panchayat and the estimated cost incurred for generation of one personday depended on the amount allocated in a particular year and the type of the assets created during the period.

(vii) The estimated number of persons who could be fully employed assuming 300 days in a year as the norm for full employment, shows that about 9 per cent more persons got employment in the M.B Block thanin the R.M. Block.

Assetwise Employment Generation under the Scheme

In this section, an attempt has been made to study the assetwise employment generation during the reference period in the two Blocks. Table 8.2 depicts the position in this regard.

Let us take the M.B Block first. It may be seen from column 3 of the table that of the total persondays generated during 1990-91 in the sampled panchayats, 31.76 per cent were generated in the form of Kachha roads, 64.71 per cent in the form of Khadanjas, 3.09 per cent in the form of Padanjas and 0.45 per cent in that of culverts. It means well over 90 per cent of the persondays were created through creation of khadanjas and kachha roads. Looking at the employment level of the various target groups assetwise we find that the share of the SCs in the total persondays generated by kachcha roads was 68.06 per cent and that of the others 31.94 per cent Women's share of the persondays generated through this activity was 1.85 per cent while that of the landless was 83.75 per cent. Under khadanjas the share of the SCs was 73.19 per cent and that of the others was 26.81 per cent, which was less than their share under kachha roads. Women's share under this asset was 121 per cent higher than their share under

Table 8.2 : Assetwise Employment Generation under the Yojana

S. No.	Name of Assets	1990-91					1991-92					1992-93				
		Total Emp.	SC	Others	Women	Landless	Total Emp.	SC	Others	Women	landless	Total Emp.	SC	Others	Women	Landless
1	2	3	4	5	6	7	8	9	10	11	12	13	14	15	16	17
	M.B. Block															
1.	Kachha	2345.00	1596.00	749.00	43.00	1964.00	1493.00	1062.00	431.00	142.00	1142.00	2800.00	2204.00	596.00	648.00	2220.00
	Road	(31.76)	(68.06)	(31.94)	(1.85)	(83.75)	(36.32)	(71.14)	(28.86)	(9.48)	(76.51)	(31.59)	(78.71)	(21.29)	(23.14)	(79.29)
2.	Khadanja	4778.00	3497.00	1281.00	195.00	3926.00	2073.00	1320.00	753.00	159.00	1560.00	2312.00	1668.00	644.00	—	1621.00
		(64.71)	(73.19)	(26.81)	(4.09)	(82.16)	(50.43)	(63.66)	(36.34)	(7.69)	(75.26)	(31.04)	(72.14)	(27.86	—	(70.10)
3.	Padanja	228.00	160.00	68.00	—	164.00	265.00	178.00	87.00	9.00	196.00	503.00	295.00	208.00	—	398.00
		(3.09)	(70.18)	(29.82)	—	(71.93)	(6.45)	(67.29)	(32.71)	(3.39)	(73.90)	(6.75)	(58.56)	(41.44)	—	(79.19)
4.	School/	—	—	—	—	—	280.00	232.00	48.00	—	260.00	250.00	220.00	30.00	—	205.00
	Panchayat	—	—	—	—	—	(6.81)	(82.86)	(17.14)	—	(92.86)	(3.36)	(88.00)	(12.00)	—	(82.00)
	Building															
5.	Land	—	—	—	—	—	—	—	—	—	—	431.00	355.00	76.00	—	346.00
	Development	—	—	—	—	—	—	—	—	—	—	(5.79)	(82.37)	(17.63)	—	(80.28)
6.	Flood/Water	—	—	—	—	—	—	—	—	—	—	396.00	326.00	70.00	—	318.00
	Control	—	—	—	—	—	—	—	—	—	—	(5.32)	(82.37)	(17.63)	—	(80.28)

[contd..]

Table 8.2 (contd.)

S. No.	Name of Assets	1990-91 Total Emp.	SC	Others	Women	Landless	1991-92 Total Emp.	SC	Others	Women	landless	1992-93 Total Emp.	SC	Others	Women	Landless
1	2	3	4	5	6	7	8	9	10	11	12	13	14	15	16	17
	M.B. Block															
7.	Village Tank/ Well	—	—	—	—	—	—	—	—	—	—	—	—	—	—	—
8.	Culvert	33.00	22.00	11.00	—	24.00	—	—	—	—	—	494.00	418.00	76.00	—	384.00
		(0.45)	(66.67)	(33.33)	—	(72.73)	—	—	—	—	—	(6.63)	(84.62)	(15.38)	—	(77.73)
9.	Others	—	—	—	—	—	—	—	—	—	—	263.00	178.00	85.00	—	202.00
		—	—	—	—	—	—	—	—	—	—	(3.53)	(67.54)	(32.46)	—	(76.96)
10.	Total	7384.00	5275.00	2109.00	238.00	6078.00	4111.00	2792.00	1319.00	255.00	3158.00	7449.00	5664.00	1785.00	648.00	5694.00
		(100.00)	(71.44)	(28.56)	(3.22)	(82.31)	(100.00)	(67.92)	(32.08)	(6.20)	(76.82)	(100.00)	(76.04)	(23.96)	(8.70)	(76.44)
	R.M. Block															
1.	Kachha	2747.00	2294.00	453.00	—	2054.00	4146.00	3229.00	917.00	—	3229.00	2557.00	2170.00	387.00	—	2312.00
	Road	(46.99)	(83.52)	(16.48)	—	(74.76)	(78.91)	(77.88)	(22.12)	—	(77.88)	(49.32)	(84.87)	(15.13)	—	(90.42)
2.	Khadanja	2208.00	1691.00	517.00	—	2151.00	235.00	190.00	45.00	—	150.00	1497.00	991.00	506.00	—	1251.00
		(37.77)	(76.59)	(23.41)	—	(76.59)	(4.47)	(80.85)	(19.15)	—	(63.83)	(28.87)	(66.21)	(33.79)	—	(83.57)
3.	School/	147.00	135.00	12.00	—	135.00	621.00	417.00	204.00	—	402.00	209.00	110.00	99.00	—	209.00
	Panchayat	(2.51)	(91.84)	(8.16)	—	(91.84)	(11.82)	(67.15)	(32.85)	—	(64.63)	(4.03)	(52.63)	(47.37)	—	(100.00)
	Building															

[contd..]

Table 8.2 (contd.)

S. No.	Name of Assets	1990-91					1991-92					1992-93				
		Total Emp.	SC	Others	Women	landless	Total Emp.	SC	Others	Women	Landless	Total Emp.	SC	Others	Women	Landless
1	2	3	4	5	6	7	8	9	10	11	12	13	14	15	16	17
	R.M. Block															
4.	Padanja	591.00	395.00	196.00	—	424.00	—	—	—	—	—	187.00	144.00	43.00	—	154.00
		(10.11)	(66.84)	(33.76)	—	(71.74)	—	—	—	—	—	(3.61)	(77.06)	(22.94)	—	(82.11)
5.	Land	—	—	—	—	—	—	—	—	—	—	536.00	481.00	55.00	—	481.00
	Development	—	—	—	—	—	—	—	—	—	—	(10.34)	(89.74)	(10.26)	—	(89.74)
6.	Flood/ Water Control	—	—	—	—	—	—	—	—	—	—	—	—	—	—	—
7.	Village Tank/ Well	—	—	—	—	—	—	—	—	—	—	—	—	—	—	—
8.	Culvert	—	—	—	—	—	—	—	—	—	—	199.00	160.00	39.00	—	160.00
		—	—	—	—	—	—	—	—	—	—	(3.84)	(80.40)	(19.60)	—	(80.90)
9.	Others	153.00	102.00	51.00	—	102.00	252.00	215.00	37.00	—	215.00	—	—	—	—	—
		(2.62)	(66.35)	(35.65)	—	(66.35)	(4.80)	(85.32)	(14.68)	—	(85.32)	—	—	—	—	—
10.	Total	5846.00	4617.00	1229.00	—	4830.00	5254.00	4051.00	1213.00	—	3996.00	5185.00	4056.00	1129.00	—	4531.00
		(100.00)	(78.98)	(19.31)	—	(82.62)	(100.00)	(77.10)	(22.90)	—	(76.06)	(100.00)	(78.23)	(21.77)	—	(87.38)

Figures in Parentheses show percentage

kachha roads. Under padanjas the share of the SCs decreased as compared to khadanjas while that of the others increased. But women had no share in the employment generated by creation of this asset. In the case of culverts the share of the SCs further decreased reducing of others increased the share of the landless labourers also decreased from its level in the case of kachha roads and khadanjas. But it increased from their share in employment generation through padanjas. Here also women did not find place.

During, 1991-92, of the total persondays generated, 36.32 per cent were generated through kachha roads, 50.43 per cent through khadanjas, 6.45 per cent through padanjas and 6.81 per cent through creation of schools and panchayat building. The share of the SCs in the total persondays generated through kachha roads was 71.14 per cent while that of others was 28.86 per cent. The share of women was 9.48 of the total persondays generated through kachcha roads and that of the landless was 76.51 per cent. In the creation of khadanjas share of the SCs was about 11 per cent, lower but that of others has increased by about 26 per cent from its level under kachcha roads. The shares of the women and the landless labourers also come down under the creation of khadanjas from those in that of the kachha roads. Under the construction of school/panchayat buildings, the share of SC increased while that of others decreased. Of the total persondays generated under this head, the landless accounted for as much as 92.86 per cent. No women got employment in the creation of this asset. The share of the SCs in the total employment generated in the creation of Padanjas was 67.29 per cent while that of the woman was 3.39 per cent. The share of the landless labourers under this head was about 74 per cent.

If we compare this year's results with those of the previous year we find that the share of the SCs and others declined slightly while that of the women increase. The share of the landless showed a decline in this year.

During 1992-93, of the total number of persondays generated, 31.59 per cent were generated through construction of Khadanjas, 31.04 per cent through construction of Khadanjas, 6.75 per cent through construction of padanjas, 3.36 per cent through school/panchayat buildings, 5.79 per cent through land development, 5.32 per cent through flood/

water control, 6.63 per cent through construction of culverts the rest through creation of other assets. During this year asset creations was diversified with as many as 8 types of assets, being created while during the previous years only 4 types of assets being created. In this year, construction of Khadanja was not a dominating activity. Its place was taken over by creation of other types of assets as the table shows. The share of the SCs in the employment generated through creation of school/Panchayat buildings land development, flood control and culverts was above 80 per cent while in the case of kachha roads and khadanjas it was 70 per cent. Their share in the employment generated through creation of padanjas and other assets was 58.56 and 67.54 per cent, respectively. The share of the others ranged from 12 per cent to 32 per cent women got employment only in the construction of kachha roads where their share of the total employment generated was about 23 per cent. The share of the landless in the employment generated through the various assets ranged from 70.10 per cent to 82 per cent.

Now let us have a look at the employment situation in the R.M. Block. Here, during 1990-91, of the total persondays generated, 46.99 per cent were generated through kachha roads, 37.77 per cent through khadanjas, 10.11 per cent through padanjas, 2.51 per cent through school/panchayat building and 2.62 per cent through other type of assets. It means more than 90 per cent of the total persondays were generated though construction of kachha road khadanja and padanjas. As regards employment of the target groups asset wise, we find that in the case of kachcha roads, the SCs share in the total employment generated was 83.52 per cent as against 16.48 per cent of the others. The share of the landless labourers in the total persondays generated through this activity was 74.76 per cent. The share of the SCs in the case of khadanjas was about 77 per cent and it is interesting to note all of those who got employment were landless labourers. In the case of padanjas the share of the SCs was about 67 per cent and the rest was that of the others. The share of the SCs in the construction of school/panchayat building, was more than 90 per cent and all were landless labourers. Their share in other types of assets created was 66.35 per cent and there also all were the landless labourers.

During 1991-92, of the total persondays generated, 78.91 per cent were generated through kachha roads, 4.47 per cent through khadanja and the rest through construction of school/ panchayat building and other assets. During this year, less persondays were created through construction of khadanjas in the comparison to the previous year as the table shows. Assetwise, the share of the SCs in the total employment generated ranged between about 67 per cent and about 85 per cent while the share of the landless ranged between 66 per cent and 92 per cent. If we compare employment position of this year with the previous year we find that share of the SCs has come down and that of others has increased. In the case of the landless labourers also the share in this year has declined.

During 1992-93, of the total persondays generated, 49.32 per cent were generated through kachha roads, 28.87 per cent through khadanjas 3.61 per cent through padanjas 10.34 per cent through land development and the rest through creation of other types of assets. During this year, the share of the construction of Kachha roads, padanjas and khadanjas together was about 80 per cent. The share of the SCs in the total employment generated through all the assets ranged between 52.63 per cent (school buildings) and 84.07 per cent (kachha roads). The share of the landless labour ranged between 80.90 per cent and 100 per cent of the 209 persondays generated through construction of school buildings 52.63 per cent went to the SCs and the rest for others. But all were landless labourers as the table shows.

A comparative study of the employment generated through the creation of various assets reveals the following:

(a) Major part of the employment generated during the three years in both the Blocks was through construction of kachha roads, khadanjas and pandanjas. But their preponderent share has been reducing year after year as the pattern of the assets created shows. It means the people have been increasingly substituting these three activities by construction of school building, water development and other types of assets.

(b) The SCs were the main beneficiaries of the employment generated in both the Blocks. Comparatively, their share was more in the R.M. Block than in the M.B

Block. However, their share has also been decreasing year after year. This trend is sharper in the R.M. Block than in the other M.B. Block

(c) More than 75 per cent of the beneficiaries, both SCs and non SCs, were landless labourers. In respect of some assets they were the only beneficiaries.

(d) Women got employment benefits only in the M.B Block. Here also they did not get employment in the creation of all types of assets. They got it only in the construction of kachha roads, khadanjas and padanja.

Employment Status of the Sampled Beneficiaries

Table 8.3 presents the employment status of the sampled beneficiaries during the reference period, blockwise, worker

Table 8.3 : Employment status of the Beneficiaries during the reference period

(per Beneficiary)

	Average Number of Persondays Employed					
	M.B. Block			*R.M. Block*		
S. No. *Particulars*	*1990-91*	*91-92*	*92-93*	*1990-91*	*91-92*	*92-93*
Total	202.00	194.06	209.70	204.37	199.58	208.80
1. SC	206.42	207.26	214.22	208.18	210.00	213.55
2. Others	188.75	162.00	200.11	196.50	181.05	194.92
3. Women	210.67	211.00	211.00	—	—	—
4. Landless Labourers	208.92	201.25	218.03	204.37	207.06	215.78

categorywise and yearwise. In the M.B. Block, on an average worker employment (including under JRY) was 202.00 for persondays, 194.06 persondays and 209.70 persondays during 1990-91, 1991-92 and 1992-93, respectively. It means there was not much difference in the employment status of the beneficiaries in the three years. Assuming 300 persondays to be the full employment norm, all the beneficiaries were employed about 33 per cent below the full employment level.

The employment status of the SCs conforms to the overall status of the workers but it has shown a steady increasing trend as during 1990-91 it was 206.42 persondays but rose to

207.26 persondays during 1991-92 and further to 214.22 persondays during 1992-93. From 1990-91 to 1992-93 their employment status rose by about 4 per cent which is almost equal to the rise in the aggregate employment status of the workers.

For the others the employment status during 1990-91 was 188.75 persondays and declined to 162.00 persondays during 1991-92. It rose to 200.11 during 1992-93. From 1990-91 to 1992-93, the level of employment of this category rose by more than 6 per cent which is 2 per cent more than the increase in the case of the SC workers. The employment status of the women workers was a little over 210 persondays during the reference period. Although in their case, there was not much increase noticed in the employment status but it was well above the average in all the three years. One thing more, during 1991-92 the employment status of most categories of workers showed a decline from the previous year but that of the women workers went up. On an average a landless worker worked for 208.92 during 1990-91, 201.25 days during 1991-92 and 218.03 days during 1992-93. The increase in their case between 1990-91 and 1992-93 was of more than 4 per cent. It means that the employment status of those who were landless among the SCs and others not very much different from that of the SCs as a whole.

In the R.M. Block, the average number of persondays employed was 204.37, 199.58 and 208.80 during 1990-91, 1991-92 and 1992-93 respectively. Here, the increase from 1990-91 to 1992-93 was 2.17 per cent. Categorywise, the employment level for the SCs was 208.18 persondays during 1990-91, 210.00 persondays during 1991-92 and 213.55 persondays during 1991-92. It shows a increase in their employment levels. Their increase was of about 3 per cent in 1992-93 over 1990-91. In the case of the others, the employment level which was 196.50 persondays during 1990-91 came down to 194.92 in 1992-93, a reduction of about 1 per cent over the three year period. The employment status of the landless workers was 204.77 persondays during 1990-91, 207.06 during 1991-92 and 215.78 persondays during 1992-93. Here also, as in the case of the SCs a steady increase is noticed.

A comparison of the employment status of the various categories of workers in both the Blocks reveals the following:

The average worker employment status is almost similar in both the Blocks. In the case of the SCs also it almost the same in both the blocks. Similarly, in the case of the others and landless labourers the difference is negligible. Overall, the employment status of the workers during the reference period in both the Blocks was around 200 person days.

Employment Status of the sampled workers under the JRY

Table 8.4 presents the employment status of the workers under the JRY during the reference period.

Table 8.4: Employment status of the sampled Beneficiaries under the JRY

(per Beneficiary)

S. No.	Particulars	*Average Number of Persondays Employed*					
		M.B. Block			*R.M. Block*		
		1990-91	*91-92*	*92-93*	*1990-91*	*91-92*	*92-93*
	Total	36.69	34.46	34.25	13.63	12.02	12.12
1.	SC	40.97	41.44	41.36	13.82	10.31	10.47
2.	Others	23.83	17.50	19.18	13.25	15.06	16.92
3.	Women	25.67	31.00	20.50	—	—	—
4.	Landless Labourers	24.13	23.38	24.54	10.92	12.83	13.46

Let us take the M.B. Block first. In this Block, the average number of persondays a worker who employed under the JRY was 36.69 during 1990-91, 34.46 during 1991-92 and 34.25 during 1992-93. It shows a steady decline over the three years. If declined by about 6 per cent in 1991-92 from the previous year's level and about 7 per cent in the next year. Categorywise the employment level of the SC workers during 1990-91 was 40.97 persondays. It was 41.44 persondays in 1991-92 and 41.36 persondays during 1992-93. It means there was no significance change in their employment status over the period. In the case of the employment level was 25.67 persondays during 1990-91, 31.00 persondays during 1991-92 and 20.50 persondays during 1992-93. It means their status rose during 1991-92 from the previous years level but came down during 1992-93. In percentage terms, their employment status rose by about 21 per cent during 1991-92 from that in 1990-91 but came down by about 34 during 1992-93 from the 1991-92 level. If we take a view of the entire three year period we find that the women's employment status had suffered a decline over the period. Here, two things may be noted.

(a) The women's employment status is lower than the aggregate employment status and

(b) the reduction rate of employment in their case over a period of time has also been higher than that in that of all the workers.

The employment status of the other workers was 23.83 persondays during 1990-91, 17.50 persondays during 1991-92 and 19.18 persondays during 1992-93. Here also, the level during 1991-92 was lower then that in 1990-91. But it recovered during the following year. In statistical terms, it declined by about 27 per cent during 1991-92 from the 1990-91 level but rose by about 10 per cent during 1992-93. In the case of the landless, the figure for 1990-91 was 24.13 which came down to 23.38 during 1991-92 but rose to 24.54 during 1992-93.

In the R.M. Block, in aggregate terms, worker employment was 13.63 persondays during 1990-91, 12.02 persondays during 1991-92 and 12.12 persondays during 1992-93. It was less by about 11 per cent in 1992-93 than in the first year of the reference period. Let us discuss the employment status category-wise. The employment status of the SCs which was 13.82 persondays during 1990-91 came down to 10.47 persondays during 1992-93 a 24.24 per cent reduction from the base year. The average worker employment of the others was 13.82 persondays during 1990-91, 15.06 persondays during 1991-92 and 16.92 persondays during 1992-93. This shows an increasing trend. In percentage terms their level of employment rose by 27.70 per cent over the three-year reference period. In the case of the landless workers, the average was 10.92 persondays during 1990-91, 12.83 persondays during 1991-92 and 13.46 persondays during 1992-93 as the table shows. Here also, as in the case of the category of others the level has risen by 23.26 per cent from 1990-91 to 1992-93.

A comparison of the situation the in the two Blocks reveals the following:

(a) The average worker got about 12 persondays of employment in the R.M. Block as against about 34 persondays in M.B. Block.

(b) In the case of the SC workers, while the employment status in the M.B. Block remained almost the same during the reference period, in the R.M. Block it showed a decreasing trend.

(c) In the case of the others and the landless workers, the level in the M.B. Block showed a declining trend for the former and was stationery for the latter whereas in the R.M. Block both the categories showed an increasing trend.

To conclude, the level of employment depends on the type of assets created during the year. If the assets are wage-employment-oriented, the persondays generated would be more, and if they are more material component oriented the persondays generated would be less.

Average Annual Incremental Employment:

Table 8.5 presents the average number of persondays employed outside the JRY, under the JRY and their total during the reference period in both the Blocks.

In the M.B. Block, col.5 shows the net increment or decrease of employment level outside the JRY. As it indicates during 1991-92, there was a 3.45 per cent decline the this level from the previous years. But during 1992-93, it went up by about 6 per cent from the base year. Under JRY, as col.6 shows there was a 6.08 per cent reduction during 1991-92 from the level in 1990-91. During 1992-93 also the trend remained the same as there was a 6.65 per cent reduction during this year. Putting the JRY and extra-JRY employment together (col.7), we find that during 1991-92 the total employment level decreased by about 4 per cent from the previous year. But during1992-93, it could make good about 50 per cent of the reduction. This is a healthy sign because it shows an increase in the employment level during the last year of the reference period.

To conclude, what we find from the above analysis is that in this Block, employment under the JRY has been reduced by about 6 per cent which is not a healthy trend.

Table 8.5: Average Annual Incremental Employment to Beneficiaries

(per Beneficiary)

Year	*Average No. of persondays employed outside the JRY*	*Average No. of persondays employed under the JRY*	*Average persondays employed*	*Net Increase in employment outside JRY (%)*	*Net Increase in employment under JRY (%)*	*Total increase in employment level (based on col. 4)*
1	2	*3*	*4(2+3)*	*5*	*6*	*7*
M.B. Block						
1990-91	165.31	36.69	202.00	—	—	—
1991-92	159.60	34.46	194.06	(–)3.45	(–)6.08	(–)3.93
1992-93	175.45	34.25	209.70	6.13	(–)6.65	3.81
R.M. Block						
1990-91	193.74	13.63	204.37	—	—	—
1991-92	187.56	12.02	199.58	(–)2.34	(–)3.19	(–)2.34
1992-93	196.68	12.12	208.80		2.17	11.52

In the R.M. Block the employment level outside the JRY during 1991-92 showed a decline of about 3 per cent from 1990-91. However, during 1992-93, it showed an increase of 2 per cent over the base year. In this case of JRY employment level, both in 1991-92 and 1992-93 there was a reduction of about 11 per cent from the level in 1990-91 as col.5 of the table shows. Taking the JRY and extra JRY employment together we find that the employment situation had improved as the reduction level had come down to 2.34 in 1991-92 and had ever turned into increment in the following year although was very little the extent.

Comparing the results of both the Blocks we find that:

(a) The employment level onside the JRY in both the Blocks had decreased during 1991-92 from 1990-91. However the reduction was sharper in M.B. Block than in the R.M. Block. But during 1992-93, in both the Blocks it showed an upward trend although here again the trend was sharper in the M.B. Block.

(b) The employment situation under the JRY was very grim in both the blocks with the employment level in both showing a decline during 1991-92 as well as during 1992-93. But the reduction rate in the R.M. Block was just double of that in the M.B. Block.

(c) As regards the overall level of employment, in both the Blocks it showed a decline during 1991-92 but the decline was sharper in the M.B. Block than in the other Block. During 1992-93 the trend had reversed in both the Blocks but the reversal had nothing to do with JRY.

Opportunity Cost of Employment Generation Under the JRY

An attempt has also been made to find out whether any worker had sacrified/foregone his/her work to get employment under the JRY. In other words, was there any opportunity cost involved in the employment creation under the JRY. Table 8.6 shows the opportunity cost of employment generation under the scheme. Col. 2 gives the average number of persondays employed under JRY. Col. 3 shows the average number of persondays sacrified to get employment under it

Table 8.6: Opportunity cost of employment generation under JRY

Year	*Average no. of personday employed under JRY*	*Average no. of personday sacrificed to get employment his JRY*	*Net Employment Benefits to beneficiaries from JRY*
M.B. Block			
1990-91	36.69	25.94	10.75
1991-92	34.46	24.79	9.67
1992-93	34.25	24.00	10.25
R.M. Block			
1990-91	13.63	5.29	8.34
1991-92	12.02	3.10	8.92
1992-93	12.12	2.45	9.67

and Col. 4 the net employment benefits to the beneficiaries from employment under the JRY. As discussed earlier, an average worker in the M.B. Block got 36.69 persondays equivalent of employment during 1990-91, 34.46 persondays during 1991-92 and 34.25 persondays during 1992-93. But as Col. 3 shows during 1990-91 an average worker had forgone 25.94 persondays employment to get the 36.69 persondays employment under the JRY. Thus, the net benefit the worker got was 10.75 persondays. Similarly, during 1991-92 the average worker got net benefit of 9.67 persondays only and he got 10.25 persondays, benefit during 1992-93. It means on an average a worker got 10 persondays net employment during the reference period.

In the case of the R.M. Block, an average worker got 8.34 persondays net employment benefit during 1990-91, 8.92 persondays during 1991-92 and 9.67 persondays during 1992-93. Here, an average worker got about 9 persondays net employment benefit.

In the M.B. Block during 1990-91, 12.50 per cent workers have preferred JRY work the their usual work they were doing. Of them, 8.33 per cent were from the SC category and 4.17 per cent were from the other categories. Of the total 4.17 per cent were landless. There was no woman worker who sacrified her normal work to get JRY employment. During 1991-92 the position remained the same. But during 1992-93, the proportion of such worker was 13.21 per cent. Of the total 9.43 per cent were from the SC category. 3.77 per cent from other categories, 1.89 per cent were women and 5.66 per cent landless workers. It means the number of workers showing preference too JRY work had increased.

In the R.M. Block, during 1990-91, there were 10.70 per cent workers who had preferred work under the JRY. Of them, 4.08 were SCs and 6.12 were others. Of the total, 4.08 per cent were landless labourers. During 1991-92, the number of such persons remained the same but thier pattern had changed because 2 per cent of them were from the SCs and 8 per cent of them were from other categories. All of them were landless workers. During 1992-93, the number of such persons was 7.84 and all belonged to the other category of workers who were also landless workers.

The reasons they gave for preferring JRY work in comparison to other work were among others, more wages and their timely payment, light work, and freedom of work. One women who preferred JRY work was casually working as furnace worker. That work was not apropriate for her as she was an asthamatic patient. That is why she preferred JRY work.

Distance of work sites from the workers' residence

Table 8.7 shows the distance of work sites from the workers residences in both the Blocks. The distance categories are four viz, less than 1 km., 1-2 km, 2-3 kms and 3-4 kms. The responses of the workers Blockwise was as follows.

Table 8.7: Distance of work sites from the precedence of the works

		Place of Work			
		M.B. Block		*R.M. Block*	
Sl. No.	*Distance (Kms)*	*No. of Workers*	*Percentage*	*No. of Workers*	*Percentage*
1	2	3	4	5	6
1.	1	1	0.67	—	—
2.	1-2	147	98.66	140	93.33
3.	2-3	1	0.67	—	—
4.	3-4	—	—	10	6.67

In the M.B. Block of the total workers 0.67 per cent worked within a km. of their residences, 98.66 per cent within 1-2 km from their residences and 0.67 within 2-3 km from their residences.

In the case of the R.M. Block, of the total workers, 93.33 per cent worked within 1-2 km from their residences, and the rest 6.67 worked within 3-4 kms of thie residences. Herc, none of the workers had his place of work either within 1 km of his residence or 2-3 kms away from it.

The results of both the Blocks in this regard show that almost all workers worked within 1-2 kms of their residences in the M.B. Block as against 93.33 per cent in the R.M. Block. Secondly, in the M.B. Block, none of the workers worked within 3-4 km residences of their whereas in the R.M. Block about 7 per cent of them worked within this distance.

Besides the distance from residence, the facilities available at the work sites for the workers were also a part of the enquiry (Table 8.8). The facilities asked about were thatched or other types of temporary stands for resting, drinking water and child care facilities. It was found that when the work was undertaken within a village, none of these facilities were required. But when it was undertaken outside the village, none of them were available or provided under the scheme while as per JRY the guidelines "arrangement for providing facilities like drinking water, rest sheds for the workers and creches for the children coming with working mothers should be made. Expenditures involved for providing these facilities should be met out of the non-wage components under the Yojana".

Besides, the workers were asked whether they got employment in lean season. In reply to this question, 87.92 per cent of the respondents in the M.B. Block reported that they got employment in the lean season while 91.33 per cent of the respondents in the R.M. Block gave this answer. In other words, JRY works was better planned in the latter Block than in the former Block.

Table 8.8: Facilities avaailable at work site

S. No.	Particulars	M.B. Block			R.M. Block		
		1990-91	91-92	92-93	1990-91	91-92	92-93
1.	Thatched Temporary Stand (%)	85.40	89.60	86.80	100.00	96.00	100.00
2.	Drinking Water (%)	100.00	97.90	98.10	100.00	96.00	100.00
3.	Childcare Facilities (%)	—	—	—	—	—	—
4.	Others (%)	—	—	—	—	—	—
5.	Whether Condition/ Life of the House hold has been improved after taking employment under JRY.	93.80	97.90	92.50	100.00	98.00	100.00

Summing up

To conclude, of the total persondays created under the Yojana in the sampled GPs, more than 70 per cent went to the SC workers. Of the total beneficiaries under the scheme, about 80 per cent in both the Blocks were landless workers and about 6 per cent were women workers. But the latter were only in the M.B.Block. In the other Block, no woman got employment under the JRY scheme. Assetwise, the maximum employment was generated through construction of kachha roads, khadanjas and padanjas in both the Blocks. The employment level of the beneficiaries, including employment under the JRY was about 200 persondays in a year. The JRY contribution to the total employment of workers was about 15 per cent in the M.B. Block and 7 per cent in the R.M. Block. However, the average annual incremental ratios show a decreasing trend. Keeping in view the opportunity cost of employment generation it was found that the net contribution of the scheme for average beneficiary was about 5 per cent in the M.B. Block and 4 per cent in the R.M. Block. The reasons for preferring JRY employment were, among others, easier work, freedom of work and timely payment of wages. Most of the work under the scheme in both the Blocks was carried out within a distance of 1-2 km. from the workers residences. Facilities like drinking water, rest sheds etc. were not provided even when they were necessary.

9

IMPACT OF JRY ON INCOMES OF THE BENEFICIARIES

Introduction

In this chapter the annual incomes of the workers from different sources, contribution of the JRY in them and the pattern of wage payment under the scheme have been discussed.

Annual Income of the Beneficiaries:

Table 9.1 shows the of incomes of the beneficiaries from different sources both yearwise and Blockwise. In the M.B. Block the average annual income from all sources during 1990-91 was Rs. 7611.27. It was Rs 9349.06 during 1991-92 and Rs. 10823.65 in the following year. It means that there was a continuous increase in the income of the workers over the three year period. Looking at the picture activitywise, we find no uniform trend as in some cases it showed an increase while in others it declined. The income from farm activities increased during 1991-92 from the 1990-91 level but came down during 1992-93 on the other hand, the income from animal husbandry showed a constant increase. Similar was the case with income from JRY. Service activity did not contribute to the workers' family income during 1990-91 and 1991-92 but 1992-93 it made a contribution. Free collection of goods made same contribution in all the three years. The income from trade and business was Rs 3200.00 during 1990-91 and came down to Rs 1500 during 1991-92 but rose

Table 9.1: Average Annual Income of Beneficiaries

(per Beneficiaries)

S. No.	Source	M.B. Block 1990-91	M.B. Block 1991-92	M.B. Block 1992-93	R.M. Block 1990-91	R.M. Block 1991-92	R.M. Block 1992-93
1.	Average Income all sources (Rs.)	7611.27	9349.06	10823.65	6991.43	8396.40	9534.10
2.	Income from :						
(i)	Farm Activities	1956.82	2781.67	2105.77	1366.67	2071.43	1938.46
(ii)	Animal Husbandry	1230.00	1252.17	1581.54	1063.41	1305.41	1585.37
(iii)	Wage From JRY	1179.71	1317.87	2049.34	406.53	460.20	531.25
(iv)	Other wages	4848.52	6115.11	6612.40	5177.55	6220.00	6761.67
(v)	Services	—	—	4865.50	—	—	—
(vi)	Free Collection & above	1800.00	1800.00	1800.00	—	—	1000.00
(vii)	Trade and Business	3200.00	1500.00	1666.67	3000.00	3600.00	3700.00
(viii)	Remittances	1450.00	1400.00	1816.67	1100.00	1633.33	1500.00
(ix)	Others	500.00	600.00	9550.00	—	—	—

to Rs. 1666.67 during 1992-93. Income from remittances was Rs 1450.00 during 1990-91 and declined to Rs 1400.00 during 1991-92 but again raised to Rs. 1816.67 during 1992-93. Income from other sources which was Rs. 500.00 during 1990-91 rose to Rs. 600.00 during 1991-92 and further to Rs. 9550.00 next year.

In the R.M. Block, the average annual income of a beneficiaries during 1990-91 was 6991.93, which went upto Rs. 8396.40 during 1991-92 and further to Rs. 9554.10 during 1992-93. The income from farm activities increased from Rs. 1366.67 during 1990-91 to Rs 2071.43 during 1991-92 but decreased to Rs. 1938.46 during 1992-93. Income from animal husbandry showed an increasing trend over the three year period as did that under the JRY. There was no income from services in this Block nor did free collection of goods contribute anything except in 1992-93. Income from trade and business also showed an increasing trend from 1990-91 to 1992-93 but the contribution of remittances which was Rs. 1100.00 during 1990-91 and rose to Rs. 1633.33 during 1991-92 came down to Rs. 1500 during the following year. There was no income from other sources in this Block over the three year period.

A comparison of the income the pattern in two Blocks reveals the following :

(a) The average annual income of the beneficiaries in both the blocks showed an increasing trend but the rate of increase was higher in the M.B. Block than in the R.M. Block. In the former it was about 23 per cent higher in 1991-92 than 1990-91 and in 1992-93 it was about 42 per cent more than in the base year. As against it in the latter Block, the income increased by about 20 per cent between 1990-91 and 1991-92 and by about 36 per cent between 1992-93 and the base year.

(b) Income from farm activities, an animal husbandry and other wages indicated increasing trend in both the Blocks.

(c) The income from the JRY had also been increasing in both the Blocks.

(d) There was no contribution from services in the R.M. Block but in the M.B. Block, this area of activities made a contribution during 1992-93.

Share of JRY to the total Income of Beneficiaries:

Table 9.2 presents the contribution of the JRY *vis-a-vis* that the other sources to the total income of the workers in both the blocks during the reference period. Col. 2 shows the annual income from the other source and col. 3 gives the JRY's contribution, column 4 shows the average total income of the beneficiaries column 5 the JRY contribution to the total income, col.6 the incremental income from the other sources and col. 7 the incremental income from the JRY.

As column 5 shows, in the M.B. Block during 1990-91, of the total income of the beneficiaries 15.50 per cent was contributed by the wages earned under the JRY. During 1991-92, their contribution had come down by about 5 per cent from the previous year. However, during 1992-93, it went up by about 34 per cent to about 19 per cent of the total income.

If we look at column 6 of the table we find that the incremental income from other sources had increased by about 25 per cent between 1990-91 and 1991-92 by about 36 per cent between 1990-91 and 1992-93. In the case of the JRY income

Table 9.2: Share of JRY income to the Total income of Beneficiaries

(per Beneficiary)

Year	*Average income from other sources (Rs.)*	*Average annual income from JRY (Rs.)*	*Average total income (Rs. 2+3)*	*Year wise Contribution of JRY in total income (%)*	*Incremental income from other sources (Rs.)*	*Incremental income from JRY (Rs.)*
1	2	3	4	5	6	7
M.B. Block						
1990-91	6431.56	1179.71	7611.27	15.50	—	—
1991-92	8031.19	1317.87	9349.06	14.10	1599.44 (24.87)	138.16 (11.71)
1992-93	8774.31	2049.34	10823.65	18.93	743.12 (36.43)	869.63 (73.72)
R.M. Block						
1990-91	6584.90	406.53	6991.43	5.81	—	—
1991-92	7936.20	460.20	8396.40	5.48	1351.30 (20.52)	53.67 (13.20)
1992.93	9002.85	531.25	9534.10	5.57	1066.65 (36.72)	124.72 (30.68)

Figures in Parantheses show the percentages.

there was an increase of about 12 per cent between 1990-91 and 1991-92 and about 74 per cent between the base year and the last year of the reference period. It means that the income from both the sources had increased. But the increase in the case of JRY was more than in that the income from the other sources.

In the R.M. Block, during 1990-91, the income from the JRY constituted 5.81 per cent of the total income of the beneficiaries while during 1991-92, its share was 5.48 per cent of the total income. It mean a reduction of about 6 per cent from the previous year. During 1992-93, the JRY income formed 5.57 per cent of the total income of the beneficiaries which was about 2 per cent more than in the previous year. However, compared with the position in the base year, it showed a reduction of about 4 per cent.

The income from the other sources during 1992-93, increased by about 21 per cent from the previous year's level and by about 37 per cent from the 1990-91 level while that from the JRY registered an increase by about 13 per cent during 1991-92 over the previous year. The increase between 1992-93 and the base year was of about 31 per cent. It means that the rate of increase in income under JRY was more than that of the other incomes, in this Block.

A comparison of the impact of JRY on the income of the beneficiaries shows that the contribution of the scheme JRY has been higher in the M.B. Block than in the R.M. Block. The incremental rate of the income has also been higher in the former than in the latter Block.

Besides studying the contribution of the JRY to the total income of the beneficiaries an attempt has also been made to examine the net income contribution of the JRY to their income. This is based on the net employment benefit to an average beneficiary from the scheme calculated by after deducting the average number of persondays sacrificed by him to get the JRY employment. The net employment benefit has been converted into monetary terms by multiplying the net persondays with average wage rate. The average wage rate here included the wage rates for both skilled and non skilled workers.

Table 9.3 presents the net income benefit to workers from JRY. It shows this benefit in the M.B block at Rs 345.74

Table 9.3 : Net income contribution to beneficiaries from JRY

(per Beneficiary)

Year	*Average No. persondays employed under JRY*	*Average No. of persondays sacrified to get employed under JRY*	*Net. employment to beneficiary (No.)*	*Average wages (Rs.)*	*Average income from JRY (Rs.)*	*Average opportunity cost to income from JRY (Rs.)*	*Net Income benefit from JRY (Rs.)*
1	2	3	4	5	6	7	8
M.B. Block							
1990-91	36.69	25.94	10.75	32.15	1179.71	833.97	345.74
1991-92	34.46	24.79	9.67	38.24	1317.87	947.97	369.90
1992-93	34.25	24.00	10.25	59.83	2049.34	1435.92	613.42
R.M. Block							
1990-91	13.63	5.29	8.34	29.83	406.53	157.80	248.73
1991-92	12.02	3.10	8.92	38.29	460.20	118.70	341.50
1992.93	12.12	2.45	9.67	43.83	531.25	107.38	423.87

during 1990-91, Rs 369.90 during 1991-92 and Rs. 613.42 during 1992-93. It means about 7 per cent net increase in monetary income during 1991-92 over 1990-91 and about 66 per cent increase during 1992-93 over 1991-92. In R.M. Block, the net income benefit to the beneficiary was Rs. 248.73 during 1990-91, Rs. 341.50 during 1991-92 and Rs. 423.87 during 1992-93. It amounts to about 37 per cent increase during 1991-92 over 1990-91 and about 24 per cent increase during 1992-93 over 1991-92.

A comparison of the net income benefits to the beneficiaries in the two Blocks shows that it had been increasing in both. Also that during 1991-92 the increase was sharper in the R.M Block whereas during 1992-93 it was sharper in the M.B.Block.

Pattern of wage payment under JRY

Table 9.4 shows the pattern of wage payment and related information under the JRY. Here six aspects of wage payment viz periodicity of payment, site of wage payment, whether wages were given on market day, whether workers kept record of employment, whether they signed or give thumb impressions to get wages and whether they got wage slip are discussed both yearwise and Block wise.

In the M.B. Block, none of the workers got wages daily during the reference period except in 1991-92 when about 4 per cent of them their wages daily. All this workers got their wages fort nightly during the first two years while in the last year 94.34 per cent of them got their wages at this periodicity. Only about 2 per cent of the workers got wages monthly, that, too, only during 1992-93. None of the workers got wages half yearly.

The percentage of workers getting wages at work site, during 1990-91, 1991-92 and 1992-93 was 95.80 in the first two years and 96.20 per cent during the last year. About 98 per cent of the workers got the wages on the market day during 1990-91. Their percentage during 1991-92 and 1992-93 was hundred and a little over 98 respectively. Almost all the workers kept no record of their employment or income. For receiving the wages, 58.30 per cent of the workers gave signed receipts during 1990-91 with the number rising to 60.40 per cent during the next two years. The rest got the

Table 9.4: Pattern oof Payment under JRY

(in Percentages)

Particular	*Name of Blocks*					
	M.B. Block			*R.M. Block*		
	1990-91	*1991-92*	*1992-93*	*1990-91*	*1991-92*	*1992-93*
1	*2*	*3*	*4*	*5*	*6*	*7*
Periodicity of Payment						
Daily	—	3.77	—	—	—	—
Forthmonthly	100.00	100.00	94.34	83.70	82.00	94.10
Monthly	—	—	1.89	16.30	18.00	5.90
Six Monthly	—	—	—	—	—	—
Site of Wage Payment						
Work Site	95.80	95.80	96.20	73.50	72.00	84.30
Outside Site	4.20	4.20	3.80	26.50	28.00	15.70
Getting Wages						
Market day	97.90	100.00	98.10	79.60	82.00	90.20
Non Market day	2.10	—	1.90	20.40	18.00	9.80
Keep Employment Record						
Keeps	2.10	—	—	—	—	—
Does not keep	97.90	100.00	100.00	100.00	100.00	100.00
Receive Wages						
Signature	58.30	60.40	60.40	42.90	48.00	35.30
Thump	41.70	39.60	39.60	47.10	52.00	64.70
Wage Slip						
Yes	—	—	—	—	—	—
No.	100.00	100.00	100.00	100.00	100.00	100.00

wages by giving thumb impressions on the receipts. None of the workers got wage slips during the reference period. In the R.M. Block none of the worker got wages daily through out the reference period while 83.70 per cent 82.00 per cent and 94.10 per cent of them got thier wages for nightly during 1990-91, 1991-92 and 1992-93 respectively got their wages monthly. Like the other Block none of the workers in this Block too got wages six monthly during the reference period.

During 1990-91, of the total workers, 73.50 per cent got their wages on the work site and the rest outside it. During 1991-92, the percentage of such workers come down to 72 while during 1992-93 it went up to 84.30 per cent, as the table shows.

During 1990-91, of the total workers, 79.60 per cent got their wages on market day and this percentage went up to 82 during 1991-92 and further to 90.20 during 1992-93. None of the workers kept a record of his employment and income during the reference period. Of the total, 42.90 per cent, 48.00 per cent and 35.30 per cent of the workers got their wages by signing the receipts during 1990-91, 1991-92 and 1992-93 respectively and the rest got them by giving thumb impressions. None of the workers got wage slip throughout the reference period.

Comparing the position in the two Blocks, we find that almost 100 per cent of the workers got wages fortnightly in the M.B. Block as against about 83 per cent in the R.M. Block. Comparatively a larger number of the workers got wages at site in the M.B. Block than in the R.M. Block. In the M.B. Block almost 100 per cent of the workers got wages on the market day while it was not so in the R.M. Block. None of the workers in any of the Blocks received wage slip during the reference period.

To conclude, it may be said that the wage payment pattern and related aspects were dealt with better in the M.B. than in the R.M. Block.

Besides studying the wage payment under the JRY, an attempt has also been made to compare the JRY wage rates and what the workers expected the two sampled Blocks. Table 9.5 presents the wage rates under the JRY and the wages expected by the workers. In the M.B. Block, in case of the skilled labour the wage was Rs. 40/- per day during 1990-91 while the worker expected Rs. 60.00 per day. It means the laboures expected 50 per cent more wage then what they were getting. During 1991-92, skilled labourers were getting Rs. 60 per day but they expected 70.00 per day. Here again the expectation was about 17 per cent more than what they were getting. Similarly, during 1992-93, they got Rs. 75.00 per day, while their expectation was Rs. 80 per day. It means they were getting about 7 per cent less than their expectation. On the other hand, in the case of unskilled labour, the workers were getting Rs. 18.00 per day but they wanted Rs. 25.00 per day, which means about 38 per cent more than the amount they were getting. During 1991-92, they were getting Rs. 20.00 per day but they wanted Rs. 30.00 per day which means 50 per cent more than what they were getting. Similar was the case during 1992-93 when they expected 40 per cent more than the actual wage similar was the position as regards women. There were no difference in wages between peak season and busy season because the cropping pattern has left no difference between the two.

Exactly same were the expectations of skilled and unskilled labourers in the R.M. Block, as the table shows.

Multiple Regression Analysis: Determinants of Income of the Beneficiaries

In this section, an attempt has also been made to examine the main determinants of the income of the beneficiaries in the study area.

The determinants of the income are: Social classification of the beneficiaries, land possessed, employment under JRY, skill, number of wage earners in beneficiaries households, number of self-employed in beneficiaries' households, employment outside JRY and sex are chosen for this exercise. Income of the beneficiaries is a dependent variable and others are independent variables. A brief description of these variables is as follows: Social classification here means SCs and others. For the former code 1 and for the latter code 2 are used. Employment under JRY means number of days beneficiaries got employment under the scheme during the

Table 9.5: Expected wage rate and wage rates under JRY (*in Rs.*)

S. No.	*Wages*	*M.B. Block*			*R.M. Block*		
		1990-91	*1991-92*	*1992-93*	*1990-91*	*1991-92*	*1992-93*
1	*2*	*3*	*4*	*5*	*6*	*7*	*8*
1.	Wages under JRY						
	(a) Skilled						
	(i) Male	40.00	60.00	75.00	40.00	60.00	75.00
	(ii) Female	—	—	—	—	—	—
	(b) Unskilled	—	—	—	—	—	—
	(i) Male	18.00	20.00	25.00	18.00	20.00	25.00
	(ii) Female	18.00	20.00	25.00	—	—	—
2.	Expected Wage Rate						
	I-Plak Season						
	(a) Skilled						
	(i) Male	60.00	70.00	80.00	60.00	70.00	80.00
	(ii) Female	—	—	—	—	—	—
	(b) Unskilled	—	—	—	—	—	—
	(i) Male	25.00	30.00	35.00	25.00	30.00	35.00
	(ii) Female	25.00	30.00	35.00	25.00	30.00	35.00
	II-Off Season						
	(a) Skilled						
	(i) Male	60.00	70.00	80.00	60.00	70.00	80.00
	(ii) Female	—	—	—	—	—	—
	(b) Unskilled	—	—	—	—	—	—
	(i) Male	25.00	30.00	35.00	25.00	30.00	35.00
	(ii) Female	—	—	—	—	—	—

reference period. Skill means the workers who were skilled (assigned code 1) and those who were unskilled (assigned code 2). Number of wage earners means their number in the workers' families, number of self employed means their number in the beneficiaries households, employment outside means number of days beneficiaries got employment outside the JRY during the reference period and sex means male or female. These dependent and independent variables have been tested with the help of multiple regression in order to examine their contribution in the income of beneficiaries of the study area. It is found that the first five independent variables, namely social classification, land possessed, employment under JRY, skill and number of wage earners in beneficiaries households contributed significantly to the income of the beneficiaries and the rest, as they have made no contribution in the income of the beneficiaries, have been dropped.

Table 9.6 presents the estimated values of explanatory variables along with their'T' values. It also presents the values of 'R' square. The value of 'R' square is 0.50 which shows that 50 per cent income of the beneficiaries is explained by these five independent variables. Variable- wise the discussion is as follows:

The Beta coefficient value of social classification variable is 0.17 which is significant at 0.05 level. It shows that others (means non-SCs) contribute more in their income than the SCs. It means, there is a positive relationship between others (Non SC) and income of the beneficiaries.

Table 9.6: Determinants of Income

S. No.	*Independent Variables*	*Dependent Variables = Income*	
		Beta	*T Value*
1.	Social classification	0.17**	11.7
2.	Land possessed	0.18**	4.3
3.	Employment under JRY	0.10**	3.7
4.	Skill	–0.54*	2.4
5.	Nos. of wage earners	0.09*	2.1
	Multiple R = 0.71 R Square = 0.50		

* Significant of 0.05 level
** Significant at 0.01 level'

The Beta coefficient value of land possessed is 0.18 which is significant at .05 level. This also shows positive relationship between land possessed and income. It indicates that land distribution has a positive impact on the income of the beneficiaries and the government should implement land reform rigorously. The Beta coefficient value of employment is 0.10 which is significant at .05 level. The Beta coefficient value of skill valuable is - 0.54 which is also significant at .01 level. The minus sign shows that the trend is from unskilled to skilled. It indicates the necessity for providing skill to the beneficiaries for enhancing their income.

The Beta coefficient value of number of wage earners in household is 0.09 which is also significant at .01 level. It shows positive relationship between number of wage earners and income of the beneficiaries' household. In other words, greater the number of wage earners larger is the income of the beneficiaries' households.

The conclusion emerged from positive relationship between others (non SC) and income is that as others were having land, skill has contributed more than the SCs who did not have these attributes. Hence enhancing the income of the SCs, they should be trained secondly, land should be transferred in favour of the weaker sections particular SCs of the rural society. Thirdly, creation of employment opportunities with JRY type of interventions along with providing skill to the poorer sections of the society does not only enhance their income level but also helps in their social transformation.

Summing Up

To conclude, income from the JRY has been showing an increasing trend in both the Blocks. The share of the JRY income to the total income is higher in the M.B. Block than in the R.M. Block. The net benefits from the JRY to the beneficiaries were higher in the M.B. Block than in the R.M. Block. The wage payment pattern and related aspects were comparatively dealt better in the M.B. Block than in the other Block. The wages paid to both skilled and unskilled workers were less than their expection. It has emerged from the multiple regression analysis that those beneficiaries who were skilled and possessed land contributed more than those without these assets. Thus transfering of land to the weaker sections of society, particularly the SCs along with imparting of skills to them will not only enhance their income level but also help in their social transformation.

10

PLANNING, EXECUTION, MONITORING, EVALUATION AND AWARENESS BUILDING

Introduction

For effective implementation of the JRY, its proper planning, execution and regular monitoring and evaluation are very important. In this chapter, the mode of planning at the panchayat level, methods of execution, monitoring and evaluation are discussed. Assetwise execution, awareness about the programme and other related issues also discussed as a part of the study.

Mode of Planning of JRY at the Panchayat Level

Table 10.1 presents the mode of planning of JRY works at different points of time in two the Blocks. Let us first discuss the M.B. Block and then the R.M. Block.

When asked how many pradhans or gram panchayats were having JRY manual, only about one third of the total reported that they had it. They said what was the need to have this manual when the secretary knew all about they did their work according to his advice.

All the sampled GPs of this Block had prepared action plans of their JRY works and it is heartening to note that the plans had also been discussed in the Gram Sabha meetings. The procedure for preparing the action plan was like this: The

Table 10.1 : Mode of Planning of JRY at Panchayat Level

S. No.	Particulars	M.B. Block			R.M. Block		
		1990-91	*1991-92*	*1992-93*	*1990-91*	*1991-92*	*1992-93*
1	*2*	*3*	*4*	*5*	*6*	*7*	*8*
1.	No. of Panchayat having latest JRY Manual	2 (33.33)	2 (33.33)	2 (33.33)	1 (20.00)	1 (20.00)	1 (20.00)
2.	No. of Panchayat prepared action plan (%)	6 (100.00)	6 (100.00)	6 (100.00)	5 (100.00)	5 (100.00)	5 (100.00)
3.	No. of Panchayat where action discussed in GS	6 (100.00)	6 (100.00)	6 (100.00)	4 (80.00)	4 (80.00)	5 (80.00)
4.	Meeting frequencies of G.S. in a year	1	1	1	1 (20.00)	1 (20.00)	—
5.	Total Population of Sampled Panchayats (1991 Census)	19735	19735	19735	9135	9135	9135
6.	Total No. of persons attended G.S. meeting	1565	1546	1598	1315	1205	1100
(i)	No. of SC attended	711 (45.43)	804 (52.01)	753 (47.12)	455 (34.60)	435 (36.10)	420 (38.18)

(contd.)

Table 10.1 (contd.)

S. No.	Particulars	M.B. Block			R.M. Block		
		1990-91	1991-92	1992-93	1990-91	1991-92	1992-93
1	2	3	4	5	6	7	8
(ii)	No. of women attended	12 (0.77)	16 (1.03)	19 (1.19)	—	—	—
7.	Mode of communication						
(i)	Drum Beating	5 (83.33)	4 (66.67)	3 (50.00)	4 (80.00)	3 (60.00)	4 (80.00)
(ii)	Personal contact	1 (16.67)	2 (33.33)	3 (50.00)	1 (20.00)	2 (40.00)	1 (20.00)
(iii)	Others	—	—	—	—	—	—
8.	Interval of Panchayat held to discuss the progress of JRY						
(i)	Monthly	1 (16.67)	2 (33.33)	1 (16.67)	2 (40.00)	3 60.00)	3 (60.00)
(ii)	Bi-monthly	2 (33.33)	2 (33.33)	3 (50.00)	3 (60.00)	2 (40.00)	2 (40.00)
(iii)	Quarterly	—	—	—	—	—	—
(iv)	Half Yearly	—	—	—	—	—	—
(v)	Not regular	3 (50.00)	2 (33.33)	2 (33.33)	—	—	—

(contd.)

Table 10.1 (contd.)

S. No.	*Particulars*	M.B. Block			R.M. Block		
		1990-91	*1991-92*	*1992-93*	*1990-91*	*1991-92*	*1992-93*
1	*2*	*3*	*4*	*5*	*6*	*7*	*8*
9.	Average no. of meetings held during the year	6	5	6	8	7	9
10.	No. of Panchayat sought technical approval before execution of works	6 (100.00)	6 (100.00)	6 (100.00)	5 (100.00)	5 (100.00)	5 (100.00)
11.	Approval Agency						
(i)	DRDA	—	—	—	—	—	—
(ii)	Development Block	6 (100.00)	6 (100.00)	6 (100.00)	5 (100.00)	5 (100.00)	5 (100.00)
(iii)	Zilla Parishad	—	—	—	—	—	—
(iv)	Others	—	—	—	—	—	—
12.	Time taken for approval by Agency						
(i)	Less than 30 days	6 (100.00)	6 (100.00)	6 (100.00)	5 (100.00)	5 (100.00)	5 (100.00)
(ii)	30-60 days						
(iii)	60-90 days						
(iv)	90 and above						

Figures in Parentheses are percentages

people were informed through drum beating or personal contact that a meeting of the Gram Sabha (GS) would be held at such and such places. They assembled there and put forward their demands. All the demands placed before the assembly were listed and the listed items are prioritized. These prioritized items became the action plan. It may be mentioned here that in these meetings opposition group/groups are hardly represented. Their standard answer was "Nothing is going to happen there. The Pradhan will give benefits to his own groups". And it was found to be correct since in taking up the JRY works, the pradhans had given priority to those pockets of the villages, from where they had received maximum votes. However, it may be mentioned that the JRY guidelines that "the plan for development of villages in the jurisdiction of different village panchayats/mandals should be discussed thoroughly in the meetings of the village panchayat and the final decisions arrived at should determine the plan of work, to be taken up during a particular year" had to a great extent been implemented.

About the GS meetings it was found that only one meeting had been held during a year while as per the guidelines two meetings should compulsorily be held during a year.

The total number of persons attending the meetings has been given as item 6 in the table while item 5 denotes the total population of the sampled panchayats. A comparison of the two gives an indication of the peoples' participation in the meetings. Out of the total number of persons present at the meetings, the SCs' percentage was 45.43, 52.01, and 47.12 during 1990-91, 1991-92 and 1992-93 respectively. Women's participation in these meetings was negligible as the item 6 (ii) of the table shows. They constituted a mere 0.77 per cent of the total during 1990-91, 1.03 per cent during 1991-92 and 1.19 per cent during 1992-93. This means that only about 1 per cent of the total participation were women and the meetings to formulate action plans for JRY were predominantly mens' affairs. The only redeeming feature is that women's participation rate has been showing an increasing trend giving hope that in future they will be participating in their full strength. The reservation of one third of the seats in the Panchayat Bodies for them should provide an environment for their fuller participation in the development of rural areas.

Drum beating and personal contact were the two methods used to inform the people about the date, time and place of the meetings. If we look at the picture year-wise we find that during 1990-91 the share of drum beating was 83.33 per cent which came down to 66.07 period during 1991-92 and further to 50.00 per cent during 1992-93. It means this mode of communication had been replaced by personal contact. This shows that spontaneous participation of the people in village affairs had been showing declining trend.

Coming to the executive body of the GS i.e. GP we find that during 1990-91, of the total GP meeting for JRY planning 16.67 per cent were held monthly, 33.33 per cent were held bimonthly and the rest were held irregurely. During 1991-92, one third of the meeting were held monthly, and another one third bimonthly and the rest irregularly. During 1992-93, 16.67 per cent of the meetings were held monthly, 50 per cent bimonthly and 33.33 per cent irregurely.

Item 10 of the table refers to the number of Panchayats seeking technical approval before execution of the works. It shows that all the panchayats have sought such approval. The procedure followed is like this. The Panchayat Secretary with the help of the pradhan prepares the estimates of the works to be undertaken. As we have seen kachcha roads, khandajas and padanjas are the main items of works undertaken by the panchayats under JRY and there do not require much technical help. The Junior Engineer (JE) at the Block headquarters tells the secretary that for so much area so many bricks are required and on the basis of the specifications given the secretary prepares the estimate which is later approved by the JE simply sitting at the Block headquarters. Giving an example a JE said that suppose he told the secretary that on an average 59.2 bricks were required to construct 1 sq.metre khadanja and 38 bricks were required to construct 1 sq.metre padanja would be practically impossible for him to check it the actual work had conformed to these guidelines with only one JE at the Block headquarters and the number of GPs in his Block well above 125 how could be expected to discharge this responsibility? However, if some building is to be constructed the JE is expected to check the estimates prepared by the secretary. But the cases where he actually does it are few. For all the panchayats, the approving agency is the Block

Development Office. The time taken by this agency is given as item 12 of table 10.1 which shows that all the GPs have got approval in less than 30 days. Here it may not be out of place it to mention that this approval is almost a formality. Whenever, the secretary of panchayat goes to the Block office with estimate he gets it approved by the JE.

Now, let us discuss the position in the R.M. Block. Here, it was found that only one pradhan was having the JRY Manual. Besides, it was also discovered that in addition to the Manual, he had also been receiving Gramvikas Newsletter, published by the Ministry of Rural Development of the Government of India. In all the panchayats, the action plan was prepared as well as discussed in the GS meetings except in one GP where such discussion could not take place. In the meetings held, of the total attendance, 34.60, 36.10 and 38.18 per cent was that of the SCs during 1990-91, 1991-92 and 1992-93, respectively. It shows an increasing trend of participation of this section in their development affairs. There was no woman participation in the meetings of the GS. We have already seen that in this Block not even a single woman has worked under the JRY. As regards the mode of communication, drum beating accounted for 80.00 per cent, 60.00 per cent 80.00 per cent of the total during 1990-91, 1991-92 and 1992-93 respectively. During 1990-91, 60 per cent of the meetings of GP were held bimonthly and 40 per cent were held monthly. During 1991-92, the position was just the reverse with 60 per cent of the meetings having been held monthly and 40 per cent bimonthly. During 1992-93, this position remained unchanged. Both the approving agency and the procedure followed for securing its sanction were the same as in the M.B. Block. All the JRY works of the GPs have been approved by the approving authority in less than 30 days.

A comparison of the position in the two Blocks leads to the following conclusions.

(a) The number of Pradhans having the JRY Manual was more in the M.B. Block than in the R.M. Block.

(b) The action plan of the JRY was discussed more intensively in the M.B. Block than in the other Block.

(c) Of the total persons attending GP meetings, that of the SCs was higher in the M.B. Block than it was in the R.M. Block.

(d) Women's participation was very little in the M.B. Block while it was nil in the R.M. Block.

(e) Drum beating as a mode of communication was used in both the Blocks. But it was used more in the R.M. Block than in the M.B. Block. It was also noticed that in the M.B. Block, drum beating is being replaced by personal contact.

(f) In both the Blocks, the number of meetings of the GS held irregurely was the highest.

(g) In both the Blocks, technical approval has been sought by all the panchayats. The Blocks Development Office was the approving authority.

Execution and Monitoring of JRY

Table 10.2 presents the mode of execution and monitoring of the works undertaken under the JRY in both the Blocks during the reference period.

In the M.B. Block, 35, 23 and 34 items/works were undertaken under the JRY during, 1990-91, 1991-92 and 1992-93 respectively as the table shows. All the works were executed by the panchayats. During 1990-91, about 63 per cent of the total executed works were completed on time and the rest were delayed. It was found that about 63 per cent of the delay was on the part of the GPs and the rest was due to shortage of funds. The delay on the part of the GPs was due to interference by those whose interests were adversely affected by the creation of a particular asset. For example, if a link road was to be constructed some land on its either side would have to be vacated by persons who had encroahced it. They would naturally object to construction of such a road which would delay the execution of the work. Secondly, sometimes soil had to be taken from either side for building the road and the owners of the land from which it would be taken would object to it. In such cases, the owners would have to be persuaded which would delay the creation of the assets.

During 1991-92 and 1992-93 too all the assets were completed on time as the table shows.

All works had been inspected by the block authorities. None of the works was inspected either by the DRDA or the state government. As regards the periodicity of the inspection

Table 10.2 : Execution and Monitoring of JRY Scheme

S. No.	Particulars	M.B. Block			R.M. Block		
		1990-91	*1991-92*	*1992-93*	*1990-91*	*1991-92*	*1992-93*
1	2	3	4	5	6	7	8
1.	Total no. of works Executed	35	23	34	25	19	24
2.	No. of works executed by G.P.	35 (100.00)	23 (100.00)	34 (100.00)	25 (100.00)	19 (100.00)	24 (100.00)
3.	No. of works executed by others	—	—	—	—	—	—
4.	No. of works timely completed	22 (2.86)	23 (100.00)	34 (100.00)	25 (100.00)	19 (100.00)	24 (100.00)
5.	No. of works delayed by completed	13 (13.14)	—	—	—	—	—
6.	No. of works delayed on the part of :						
	(i) G.P.	8 (62.50)	—	—	—	—	—
	(ii) DRDA/BDO	—	—	—	—	—	—
	(iii) Shortage of Funds	5 (37.50)	—	—	—	—	—
	(iv) Other reason	—	—	—	—	—	—

(contd.)

Table 10.2 (contd.)

S. No.	Particulars	M.B. Block			R.M. Block		
		1990-91	*1991-92*	*1992-93*	*1990-91*	*1991-92*	*1992-93*
1	*2*	*3*	*4*	*5*	*6*	*7*	*8*
7.	No. of Works Inspected/ Supervised by						
	(i) DRDA Officials	—	—	—	—	—	—
	(ii) Block Officials	35 (100.00)	23 (100.00)	34 (100.00)	27 (100.00)	22 (100.00)	24 (100.00)
	(iii) Zilla Parishad	—	—	—	—	—	—
	(iv) State Government	—	—	—	—	—	—
8.	No. of G.Ps in which time schedule of inspection of works were drawn byDRDA/ BDO						
	(i) DRDA	—	—	—	—	—	—
	(ii) BDO	6 (100.00)	6 (100.00)	6 (100.00)	5 (100.00)	5 (100.00)	5 (100.00)
9.	Periodicity of Schedule of Inspection						
	(i) Forthnightly	—	—	—	—	—	—
	(ii) Monthly	—	—	—	—	—	—
	(iii) Quarterly	—	—	—	—	—	—
	(v) Half yearly	—	—	—	—	—	—

(contd.)

Table 10.2 (contd.)

S. No.	Particulars	M.B. Block			R.M. Block		
		1990-91	*1991-92*	*1992-93*	*1990-91*	*1991-92*	*1992-93*
1	*2*	*3*	*4*	*5*	*6*	*7*	*8*
	(v) Irregular	6 (100.00)	6 (100.00)	6 (100.00)	5 (100.00)	5 (100.00)	5 (100.00)
10.	No. of G.P. which send progress report regularly						
	(i) DRDA						
	(ii) BDO	6 (100.00)	6 (100.00)	6 (100.00)	5 (100.00)	5 (100.00)	5 (100.00)
	(iii) Zilla Parishad						
11.	No. of G.P. having master roll	6 (100.00)	6 (100.00)	6 (100.00)	5 (100.00)	5 (100.00)	5 (100.00)
12.	Maintenace of Master roll by						
	(i) Pradhan	6 (100.00)	6 (100.00)	6 (100.00)	5 (100.00)	5 (100.00)	5 (100.00)
	(ii) Panchayat Secretary	—	—	—	—	—	—
	(iii) VVW	—	—	—	—	—	—
	(iv) Others	—	—	—	—	—	—

(contd.)

Table 10.2 (contd.)

S. No.	Particulars	M.B. Block			R.M. Block		
		1990-91	*1991-92*	*1992-93*	*1990-91*	*1991-92*	*1992-93*
1	*2*	*3*	*4*	*5*	*6*	*7*	*8*
13.	No. of G.Ps which displayed the details of works on wall/notice board	6 (100.00)	6 (100.00)	6 (100.00)	5 (100.00)	5 (100.00)	5 (100.00)
14.	No. of GPs where social audit was done	—	—	—	—	—	—
15.	No. of meeting of GS, held to apprise progres of JRY						
	(i) Once	5 (83.33)	5 (83.33)	4 (66.2)	1 (20.00)	2 (40.00)	2 (40.00)
	(ii) Twice	1 (16.67)	1 (16.67)	2 (33.33)	3 (60.00)	3 (60.00)	2 (40.00)
	(iii) None	—	—	—	1 (20.00)	—	1 (20.00)
16.	No. of G.P. where Yuvak Manda/ NGO were involved in JRY	—	—	—	—	—	—

Note: Figures in parentheses are percentage.

it was found that no schedule for it had been drawn. The inspection was therefore irregularly undertaken as the table shows. It was also found that all the GPs had been sending their reports regularly to the Block. All the GPs maintained muster rolls which were available with the pradhans who maintained them. It was also found that in all the sampled panchayats the notice boards were painted on the walls at certain places in the villages. But they had not been updated.

In one village it was found that the notice board had been placed in the house of the pradhan. When asked how many meetings of GP were held for social audit the JRY schemes. It was found that no meeting had been held for this purpose as item 15 shows. As per the JRY guidelines "in order to ensure control of the Yojana, meetings of the village panchayat shall be held every month on a fixed date, time and place to consider the issues regarding the planning, execution, monitoring and supervision of the JRY. These meetings shall be open to the village community who shall be free to raise any issue regarding implementation of the Yojana". Further, "the village assembly, to be held at least once a year, should also be kept informed about the progress of implementation of JRY and all the related issues". But these guidelines were not being implemented as the table shows. During 1990-91, only in 16.67 per cent of the GPs the GS had met twice in a year and the same was the case during 1991-92 as well however, during 1992-93, about one third of GPs the had held meetings of the GS twice in a year.

When asked whether any NGO was involved in the planning, execution and implementation of the JRY schemes the answer in all cases was in the negative as item 16 of the table shows, while, as per the JRY guidelines, "the voluntary organisations could also be involved in implementation of the programme at the district and village panchayat mandal/ levels".

Now let us discuss the position in the R.M. Block. Here, 25, 19 and 24 items of works had been undertaken during 1990-91, 1991-92 and 1992-93, respectively. All the works had been executed by the Panchayats themselves and all of them had been completed on time. The works had been inspected by the Block Development Office. No inspection had been done by the DRDA or any other agency at the district level.

The inspection by the Block office had been done irregularly. All the GPs had sent their progress reports to the Block on time and all of them had master rolls which had been maintained by the panchayats themselves. The details about the scheme such as allocation of funds cost, persondays generated etc. had been pointed on walls different places in the GP area but they had not been updated. In none of the GPs, implementation of the JRY scheme had been inspected/ evaluated by the state government or the DRDA. No meetings of the GPs were held for appraisal of the progress of the JRY while as per the JRY guidelines such meetins should have been held every month. The GS meetings were held twice during 1990-91 in 60 per cent of the GPs and the same was the position during 1991-92. However, during 1992-93 it was only in 40 per cent of the GPs that the GS had met twice in a year. No NGO was involved or participated in the planning, execution and implementation of the scheme.

If we compare the situation in the two Blocks, we find that there was not much difference in the procedures of execution and monitoring of the scheme. Both were sailing in the same boat.

Assetwise execution and completion of items of work undertaken under the JRY

Table 10.3 shows the position as regards execution and completion of different assets created under the JRY during the reference period.

In the M.B. Block, during 1990-91, 12 kachha roads were constructed. Of them, about 58 per cent were completed on time and the rest were delayed. The reasons for the delay were:(a) the difficulties faced by the panchayats in persuading those having land on either side of the roads to allow taking of soil from their land (b) lack of resources with the panchayats. In the case of khadanjas, 70 per cent of the schemes were completed on time and the rest were delayed. Here also the reasons for the delay were the same as those in the case of kachha roads. The number of padanjas created was two which were completed on time as were the rest of the assets taken up during this year. During 1991-92, 8 kachha roads, 10 khandanjas, 6 padanjas, 1 culvert and 1 other type of assets were created. All were created on time. During 1992-93, 2

Table 10.3: Assetwise Execution, Completion and reason for Delay

Sl. No.	Name of Asset	1990-91						1991-92						1992-93					
		No. of Assets	Execution Agency G.P.	Execution Agency Others	Completion of Asset Timely	Completion of Asset Delayed	Extent of locally available resources (%)	No. of Assets	Execution Agency G.P	Execution Agency Others	Completion of Asset Timely	Completion of Asset Delayed	Extent of locally available resources (%)	No. of Assets	Execution Agency G.P	Execution Agency Others	Completion of Asset Timely	Completion of Asset Delayed	Extent of locally available resources (%)
M.B. Block																			
1.	Kachha Road	12	12 (100.00)	—	7 (58.33)	5 (41.87)	100.00	8	8 (100.00)	—	8 (100.00)	—	100.00	2	2 (100.00)	—	2 (100.00)	—	100.00
2.	Khadanja	20	20 (100.00)	—	14	6	100.00	10	10 100.00	—	10 100.00	—	100.00	18	18 (100.00)	—	18	—	100.00
3.	Padanja	2	2 (100.00)		2	—	100.00	6	6 (100.00)		6 (100.00)		100.00	5	5 (100.00)		5 (100.00)		100.00
4.	School/ Panchayat Building	—	—	—	—	—		1	1 (100.00)	—	1 (100.00)	—	100.00	1	1 (100.00)	—	1 (100.00)	—	100.00
5.	Land Development	—	—	—	—	—	—	—	—	—	—	—	—	—	—	—	—	—	—
6.	Flood/Water Control	—	—	—	—	—	—	—	—	—	—	—	—	—	—	—	—	—	100.00
7.	Village Tank/Well	—	—	—	—	—	—	—	—	—	—	—	—	—	—	—	—	—	—

[contd..]

Table 10.3 (contd.)

Sl. No.	Name of Asset	1990-91						1991-92						1992-93					
		No. of Assets	Execution Agency G.P.	Execution Agency Others	Completion of Asset Timely	Completion of Asset Delayed	Extent of locally available resources (%)	No. of Assets	Execution Agency G.P	Execution Agency Others	Completion of Asset Timely	Completion of Asset Delayed	Extent of locally available resources (%)	No. of Assets	Execution Agency G.P	Execution Agency Others	Completion of Asset Timely	Completion of Asset Delayed	Extent of locally available resources (%)
	M.B. Block																		
8.	Culvert	1	1		1		100.00	1	1		1		100.00	3	3		3		100.00
			(100.00)		(100.00)				(100.00)		(100.00)				(100.00)		(100.00)		
									1		1								
9.	Others	—	—			—	—	1	(100.00)		(100.00)		100.00	3	3	—	3	—	100.00
									1		1								
								1	(100.00)		(100.00)								
	R.M. Block																		
1.	Kachha	6	6		6	—	100.00	10	10	—	10	—	100.00	5	5	—	5	—	100.00
	Road		(100.00)		(100.00)				(100)		(100)				(100.00)		(100.00)		
2.	Khadanja	9	9		9	—	100.00	5	5		5		100.00	10	10	—	10	—	100.00
			(100.00)		(100.00)				(100.00)		(100.00)				(100.00)		(100.00)		
3.	Padanja	6	6		6	—	100.00	—	—	—	—	—	—	3	3	—	3	—	100.00
			(100.00)		(100.00)				—		—			(100.00)	(100.00)				

[contd..]

Table 10.3 (contd.)

Sl. No.	Name of Asset	1990-91						1991-92						1992-93					
		No. of Assets	Execution Agency G.P.	Execution Agency Others	Completion of Asset Timely	Completion of Asset Delayed	Extent of locally available resources (%)	No. of Assets	Execution Agency G.P	Execution Agency Others	Completion of Asset Timely	Completion of Asset Delayed	Extent of locally available resources (%)	No. of Assets	Execution Agency G.P	Execution Agency Others	Completion of Asset Timely	Completion of Asset Delayed	Extent of locally available resources (%)
4.	School/ Panchayat Building	1	1 (100.00)		1 (100.00)	—	100.00	2	2 (100.00)		2 (100.00)		100.00	2	2 (100.00)		2 (100.00)		100.00
5.	Land Development	—	—	—	—	—	—	—	—	—	—	—	—	—	—	—	—	—	—
6.	Flood/Water Control	—	—	—	—	—	—	—	—	—	—	—	—	—	—	—	—	—	—
7.	Village Tank/Well	—	—	—	—	—	—	—	—	—	—	—	—	1	1 (100.00)	—	1 (100.00)	—	100.00
8.	Culvert	—	—	—	—	—	—	—	—	—	—	—	—	—	—	—	—	—	—
9.	Others	3	3 (100.00)	—	3 (100.00)	—	100.00	2	2 (100.00)	-	2 (100.00)	—	100.00	1	1 (100.00)	—	1 (100.00)	—	100.00

kachha roads, 18 khandanjas, 5 padanjas and some other assets were created. In this year also, all the schemes were completed on time.

In the R.M. Block, during 1990-91, 6 kachha roads, 9 khadanjas, 1 school, 6 padanjas and 3 other types of assets were created and all, of them were completed on time. Similarly, during 1991-92 and 1992-93, all the assets, khadanjas, padanjas, kachcha roads etc. were completed on schedule. This in itself is a record and testifies to the panchayats effective performance in this field.

Besides, in creation of all the assets during the reference period, only locally available materials were used as can be seen from col.8,14,20 of the table. Taking an overall view at may be said that it was during 1990-91 that some assets in the M.B. Block could not be completed as scheduled otherwise all the assets in both this Block assets were completed on time in the reference period.

Awareness among the Beneficiaries about the JRY

An attempt has also been made to study the level of awareness about the JRY among the beneficiaries in the two Blocks during the reference period. The data on the subject has been given in table 10.4.

In the M.B. Block, during 1990-91 about 98 per cent of the total beneficiaries were found to be aware of the scheme while during the two following years all of them showed this awareness. About the medium through which they came to know about the Yojana they were given options, namely TV, Radio, Newspapers, pradhans and others. All the beneficiaries replied that they came to know about the scheme through pradhans only. When asked whether they were aware of the provision for selecting the works under the JRY in GS meetings about 48 per cent of the beneficiaries gave an affirmation answer during 1990-91. For 1991-92 and 1992-93 this percentage was about 56 and about 60 respectively. This shows that more and more beneficiaries had been becoming aware about the Yojana. It was also found that only those beneficiaries who were aware of the yojana had participated in the meetings held to select the schemes to be undertaken under the JRY. When asked whether they attended the G.S.

Table 10.4: Awareness about the JRY

S. No.	Particulars	M.B. Block			R.M. Block		
		1990-91	*1991-92*	*1992-93*	*1990-91*	*1991-92*	*1992-93*
1	*2*	*3*	*4*	*5*	*6*	*7*	*8*
1.	Total No. of Beneficiaries	48	48	53	49	50	51
2.	Beneficiaries aware about the Schemes (%)	97.90	100.00	100.00	100.00	100.00	100.00
3.	Medium of Awareness (%)						
	(i) TV	—	—	—	—	—	—
	(ii) Radio	—	—	—	—	—	—
	(iii) Newspapers	—	—	—	—	—	—
	(iv) Pradhans	100.00	100.00	100.00	100.00	100.00	100.00
	(v) Others	—	—	—	—	—	—
4.	Beneficiaries aware about the meeting to select work under JRY (%)	47.90	56.30	60.20	30.60	39.00	39.20
5.	Beneficiaries participated in the meetings to select work under JRY (%)	47.90	56.30	60.20	30.60	32.00	39.00
6.	Beneficiaries attended the GS meetings (%)	52.10	62.50	63.00	32.70	34.00	35.30
7.	Reason for not attending meeting (%)						
	(i) Not Known	—	—	—	—	—	—
	(ii) Not Interested	30.30	22.20	32.30	9.10	12.10	9.10
	(iii) Who listen to us	69.60	72.20	67.70	78.80	78.80	84.80
	(iv) Others	—	1.40	—	12.10	9.10	6.10

meeting 52.10 per cent of the beneficiaries during 1990-91 answered in the alternative. This percentage went upto 62.50 and 63 during 1991-92 and 1992-93 respectively. Those who had not attended the meetings of the G.S. were asked the reasons for their non-participation. Their responses have been classified as (i) did not know about the meeting (ii) not interested (iii) who will listen to us and (iv) others. Of the total non-participant beneficiaries during 1990-91 about 30 per cent answered that they were not interested in the meetings and the rest 70 per cent said that they were doubtful if any body would listen to them. During 1991-92, the percentage of those who were not interested beneficiaries came down to about 22 while that of expressing doubts about the effect of their intervention rose to about 72. A very small percentage (i.e., 3. 1 per cent) had not attended the meetings due to other reasons. During 1992-93, the percentage of the not interested beneficiaries rose to about 32 while the percentage of those sceptical about the response to their intervention came down to about 68 from 72 in the previous year.

In the Block 100 per cent beneficiaries were aware of the scheme in all the three years of the reference period and all came to know about the scheme through pradhan.

About 31 per cent of the beneficiaries during 1990-91 and about 39 per cent during 1991-92 and 1992-93 aware of the provision for slecting the JRY working the meeting of GS. As may be noticed from the table this shows an increasing trend in the awareness level. Almost all those who were aware of the yojana attended the GS meetings for selection of the works under the scheme. The percentage of the beneficiaries who had attended the meetings of the GS was about 33 during 1990-91, 34 during 1991-92 and about 35 during 1992-93. As regards the reasons for not attending the meetings of GS about 9 per cent of the non-participants said that they were interested in them. About 80 per cent did not expect anybody to listen to them and about 12 per cent gave other reasons. For 1991-92, the percentage of those who were not interested rose to 12.10 while that of those who were sceptical about the response to their intervention was the some as in the previous year. The number of those other giving reasons for their non-participation came down to 9.10 per cent from 12.10 per cent in the preceding year. During 1992-93, about 9 per cent of those not attending the GS meeting were not interested, about 85 per cent did not expect anybody to listen to them and about 6 per cent gave other reasons for their absence. Here it is important to note that the number of persons who said that they were doubtful if listen to anybody would them was the largest during the first two years while during the last year it came down by about 8 per cent while, the percentage of those giving other reasons had been coming down from year to year.

A comparison of the two Blocks reveals the following:

(a) It was only in the M.B. Block in 1990-91 that a small percentage of the beneficiaries were not aware of the scheme. Otherwise, in both the Blocks, all of them had this awareness about it.

(b) All the beneficiaries in both the block came to know about the scheme through the pradhans only.

(c) The worker participation in the meeting of the GS has found to be higher in the M.B. Block than in the R.M. Block.

(d) Number of these sceptical about the effect of their intervention in the 69 meeting was more in the R.M. Block than in the M.B. Block while those not interested numbered more in the M.B. Block than in the R.M. Block. In aggregate more workers in the M.B. Block participated in the meeting than those in the R.M. Block.

Summing Up

It is clear from the above discussion that planning and monitoring of the JRY schemes have not been effectively carried out throughout the reference period in both the Blocks. Participation of women was very little in the M.B. Block and was nil in the R.M. Block. The work of the JRY in both the Blocks was executed by thc Panchayats themselves and no contractor was employed. Muster rolls were maintained. But the notice Board were found to be not updated. Had these been kept uptodate they might have made JRY a hosuehold name. The major defects in the planning and monitoring of the schemes were absence of their social audit and non involvement and non participation of the NGOs in them. The delays in execution of the schemes observed during 1990-91 in the M.B. Block were due to operational and financial reasons. All the beneficiaries were aware of the Yojana but all of them were not interested in attending the meetings held to decide the schemes. The major factors contributing to their absence were lack of interest and doubts about the effect of their intervention.

11

MILLION WELLS SCHEME

Introduction

The Million Well Scheme (MWS) was introduced during 1988-89 as a sub-scheme of the NREP and the RLEGP with the launching of the JRY during 1989-90 it was also made a sub-scheme of the new scheme and since then it has continued as such.

Salient Features of the Scheme

Objective

The scheme was launched with the objective of providing open irrigation wells, free of cost, to poor small and marginal farmers belonging to the SCs/STs and freed bounded labourers. The names of the beneficiaries have to be listed in the IRDP register of the target group. Initially, the scheme was to be confined to open wells. The scheme was to be taken up only in those areas where open well were cost effective.

Target Group

Initially, the target group were the small and marginal farmers living below the poverty line and listed in the IRDP register. Later, keeping in view its importance for the weaker sections, poor farmers belonging to the non-SC/ST households were also brought under its programmes. But the priority continued to be given to the freed bounded labourers and poor SC/STs farmers. The farmers already assisted under the minor irrigation scheme are not be given assistance under this programme.

Earmarking of Fund

Initially 15 per cent of the JRY allocation had been earmarked for this scheme. Later its share was raised to 20 per cent of the total allocation and from 1993-94 on wards 30 per cent of the total allocated funds, under the JRY have been earmarked for it so that it could be extended to the poor small and marginal farmers belonging to non-SC/ST category also.

Works to be taken up under MWS

Initially, MWS was intended for digging open wells and tube wells only or bore wells were not taken up under it. Later, digging of tube wells and bore wells were also undertaken under this scheme. Where digging of wells was not feasible due to geo-topographical factors, the allocation could be utilized for other schemes of minor irrigation like irrigation tanks and water harvesting structure and also for the development of lands belonging to small and marginal farmers. The land development was to constitute of land shaping, construction of drainage and field channels, land levelling, bunding etc.

Executing Agency

The beneficiaries themselves were to undertake the construction of the wells through their own labour and the local labour for which they would be paid. In no case was the work to be entrusted to a contractor by the project authorities.

MWS at Sampled District Level

At the Sampled District Level, the MWS is being implemented by the DRDA with the help of the following executing agencies of the state government stationed in the district.

1. Soil Conservation Office
2. Ramganga Command Ist
3. Ramganga Command IInd
4. Irrigation Construction Division
5. Rural Engineering Service
6. Block Development Office
7. Minor Irrigation Department

In the district of Saharanpur, either open well or tank is not fashionable. But since the inception of the MWS the works like water harvesting structure and development of land that is land shaping and construction of drainage and field channels have been taken up. During 1992-93 digging of bore wells had also been taken up in the district. As the bore well scheme was started during this year the data collected from the sampled GPs pertain to this year only. The total number of beneficiaries of this scheme during the year was 16.

Besides, as mentioned in the methodology, in addition to the above schemes, water harvesting structure and soil and water conservation activities have also been carried out by the different agencies at the district level as part of the MWS. Of these agencies the District Soil Conservation Office has done the maximum work in this area and has therefore been chosen for a detailed analysis.

The types of the works undertaken by this agency in different villages of the Blocks during the reference period have been taken from its office. A sample of 6 villages (5 from the M.B. Block and 1 from the R.M. Block) has been taken for detailed study. In the R.M. Block, there was only 1 village where such works were taken up. From these selected villages, 36 farmers who benefitted from the scheme have been selected at random. They have been interviewed for studying the impact of the MWS on the income and employment of the farmers.

Under the MWS mainly two types of activities have been undertaken in the sampled district; (a) Borewell, which have been undertaken during 1992-93 only (b) soil and water conservation activities continuing since inception of the scheme. Both have been discussed below.

Impact of Bore well on Employment and Income Generation of the Beneficiaries

Before discussing the impact of the Borewell on employment and income generation, let us briefly discuss the socio economic characteristics of the beneficiaries. In the M.B. Block the total number of beneficiaries among the sampled GPs were 8. All were marginal farmers belonging to SCs Community. None of them was women. Of the total farmers 3 were illiterate, 2 were literate and 3 were schooled upto primary level. In R.M. Block total number of the beneficiaries in the sampled

GPs was 8. All of them were marginal farmers belonging to the SCs. None of them was woman. Of the total farmers, 3 were illiterate, 2 were literate and 3 had schooling up to primary level. In the R.M. Block the total number of the beneficiaries in the sampled GPs was 6. All of them were marginal farmers belonging to the SCs. Of the total 5 were literate and one had been to school upto the primary standard.

None of the beneficiaries was woman in both the Blocks the reason being that the women did not own land and a bore well could be sanctioned the names of those only who owned land. Table 11.1 shows the impact of the bore well scheme on the employment and income generation of the beneficiaries. In the M.B. Block, the average employment level of the farmers before benefitting from the scheme was 153.71 persondays which rose to 205.14 persondays after receiving benefit as Table 11.1 shows. This is more than a 33 per cent enhancement in the employment level of the beneficiaries as a result of the scheme. As regards income the average income before receiving the benefit the scheme was Rs. 7788.57 which rose to Rs. 9321.43 after getting this benefit. It shows a 20 per cent increment in the income level of the beneficiaries under the scheme. Before the scheme they had saved nothing but after getting is benefit their average saving amounted to Rs. 257 as the table shows.

In the R.M. Blocks the average employment level of the Beneficiaries was 197.67 persondays which rose to 235.83 after benefitting under the scheme. This shows more than 13 per cent increment in their employment status. As regards income the average income which before benefitting under the scheme was Rs. 7571.67 rose to Rs. 8563.33 after receving its benefit. This also shows a more than 13 per cent increment in their income level. Here the beneficiaries could not make any saving as they used the entire increase in the income in household consumption. A comparison of the two Blocks reveals that the farmers of M.B. Block benefitted more than those of the R.M. Block both in terms of employment and those of income generation.

Impact of MWS on Capital Formation and Employment Generation

As has been mentioned earlier, the District Soil conservation

Table 11.1 : Impact of MWS (Bore well) on Employment, Income and Saving of the Beneficiaries

(per Beneficiary)

S. No.	*Particulars*	*M.B. Block*	*R.M. Block*
1	*2*	*3*	*4*
A.	Employment (No. of days)		
1.	No. of Beneficiaries	8	6
2.	Employment level before the scheme	153.71	197.67
3.	Employment level after the scheme	205.14	235.83
4.	Net Increase	51.43 (33.46)	38.17 (19.31)
B.	Income (Rs.)		
1.	Income before the scheme	7788.57	7571.67
2.	Income after the scheme	9321.43	8563.33
3.	Net Increase	1532.86 (19.68)	991.67 (13.10)
C.	Saving (Rs.)		
1.	Saving before	Nil	Nil
2.	Saving after	257.14	Nil
3.	Net increase	257.14 (100.00)	Nil

Figures in Parentheses show the Percentages.

office (DSCO) has been chosen as the agency for a detailed analysis of the position on this front. The work done by this agency in the district as well as in the two sampled Blocks has been collected and studied. The works undertaken under the programme by the agency are:

(i) Construction of dugouts

(ii) Construction of tanks

(iii) Levelling of land

(vi) Construction of drainages

(v) Bunding

(vi) Tree Plantation

It may be mentioned here that participation of the Gram Panchayats or people in these activities has been nil. The procedure for undertaking the various activities was like this: The District Soil Conservation Office (DSCO) surveyed the area to find out that what types of activities could be taken up in its various parts in order to conserve both water and soil. It submitted its proposals to the DRDA. After approval by the DRDA the DSCO would execute the scheme with the help of its field workers. These field workers would go to the affected areas to employ the labour with the help of the mate who acted as the leader of the workers. Table 11.2 presents the impact of MWS on water and soil conservation in the district in relation to the sampled Blocks.

M.B. Block

The area proposed to be treated in this Block during 1990-91, 1991-92 and 1992-93 was 317.00, 1206.00 and 779.00 hectares, respectively, which was about 33 per cent 47 per cent and 76 per cent, respectively, of the treated area of the district. The estimated cost for the proposed area was Rs. 9.08 lakhs during 1190-91, Rs. 41.31 lakh during 1991-92 and Rs. 30.65 lakh during 1992-93. The actual expenditure incurred during 1990-91 was Rs. 8.58 lakhs, Rs. 33.89 lakhs during 1991-92 and Rs. 28.25 lakhs during 1992-93. It means that the actual expenditure was about 6 per cent less than the estimated expenditure during 1991-92 and about 8 per cent less than the estimated expenditure during 1992-93. If we see the corresponding figures for the district we find that there the difference between the estimated and the actual expenditure is much larger than in the case of the M.B. Block.

The wage and non wage ratios in the M.B. Block were 95.5, 94.6 and 93:7 during 1990-91, 1991-92 and 1992-93, respectively. As per the JRY guidelines, at least 60 per cent of the allocation must be spent as wage component of the programme. But here, a little less than 100 per cent has been spent on wages. The scheme benefited 381 farmers during 1990-91 and 995 farmers during 1991-92 which is about 42 per cent and 61 per cent respectively of the total farmers benefiting from the scheme during the two years in the district. It shows the seriousness of the soil erosion problem in this Block. During 1990-91 a total of 42303 persondays were generated of which 63.13 per cent were for the SCs and 36.87 per cent were for others. About 45 per cent of the total persondays generated were for the landless labourers. Woman had been benefitted from the scheme. The corresponding figures for the district in the case of the SCs and the others were almost the same. However, at the district level share of the landless on the persondays generated was less than it was the Block level. During 1991-92, 161239 persondays were

Table 11.2: Impact of MWS on Capital Formation and Employment Generation

S.No.	Particulars	SAHARANPUR			M.B. BLOCK			R.M. BLOCK
		1990-91	1991-92	1992-93	1990-91	1991-92	1992-93	1990-91 to 1992-93
1	2	3	4	5	6	7	8	9
1.	Area proposed to be treated (ha)	953.00	2555.00	1025.47	317.00	1206.00	779.00	22.00 (2.00)
2.	Estimated cost (in Rs. lakh)	25.66	90.35	82.34	9.08	41.31	30.65	0.25 (0.30)
3.	Actual treated area (ha)	897.60 (94.19)	2359.21 (92.34)	1014.02 (98.88)	402 (126.81)	1103 (91.46)	736 (94.48)	22 (2.17)
4.	Actual Expenditure (Rs. In lakhs)	21.29 (82.57)	71.45 (79.08)	47.05 (57.14)	8.58 (94.49)	33.89 (82.04)	28.25 (72.17)	0.17 (0.36)
5.	Wage/Non Wage Ratio	91:9	91:9	91:9	95:5	94:6	93:7	78:22
6.	No. of farmers benefitted	901	1643	NA	381	995	NA	21
7.	No. of persondays generated							
(i)	Total	97017 (100.00)	324983 (100.00)	193663 (100.00)	42303 (100.00)	161239 (100.00)	79288 (100.00)	654 (100.00)
(ii)	SC	61815 (63.72)	165185 (50.82)	NA —	26707 (63.13)	82733 (51.3)	NA —	304 (46.48)
(iii)	ST	—	—	—	—	—	—	—
(iv)	Other	35202 (36.28)	159788 (49.17)	NA —	15596 (36.87)	78506 (48.69)	NA —	350 (53.52)
(v)	Landless	37960 (39.13)	81240 (25.00)	NA —	19065 (45.07)	30288 (18.78)	NA —	189 (16.67)
(vi)	Women	—	—	—	—	—	—	—

Source : Compiled from the data obtained from District Soil Conservation Office, Saharanpur.

generated in the Block, of which 51.31 per cent were generated for the SC and 48.69 per cent for others. This meant a fall of 19 per cent for the SCs from the 1990-91 level. The share of the landless was only 18.78 per cent, a decline of 58 per cent from the previous year. This shows that in this year both the SCs and the landless derived less benefit from the scheme then in the previous year. Conversely, the share of the other workers went up by about 32 per cent from the previous year's level. The picture at the district level almost resembles that the Block as the table shows.

During 1992-93, a total of 79288 persondays were generated of which the details were not available, as the table testifies.

R.M. Block

This Block had not been affected by soil erosion or land degradation and during the reference period only one drainage channel was constructed in one of its villages Jandhara. Even in this solitary case the DSCO had not been aware of the problem and it was the pradhan of the village panchayat who brought it to the Agency's notice in the Block Development Committee meeting. This is a brief background of this work.

In the R.M. Block an area of 22 hectares was treated. Total estimated expenditure was Rs. 0.25 lakhs of which only 68 per cent (Rs.0.17 lakhs) was actually spent. Wage and non wage ratio was 78:22 which was more than the prescribed norm. A total number of 21 farmers benefited from the scheme. The number of persondays generated was 654. Of which 46.48 per cent went to the SCs and 53.52 per cent to others. Of the total beneficiaries about 17 per cent were landless. As in the case of the other Block, no woman benefited from this scheme in this Block either.

A comparison of the position in the two Blocks shows (i) land degradation is severe in the M.B. Block than in the R.M. Block (iii) the wage component was higher in the M.B. Block than the R.M. Block (iii) The SCs and the landless got more employment under the scheme in the M.B. Block than in the R.M. Block.

Sidelights from field study

An attempt has also been made to evaluate the impact of the various activities under the scheme such as drainage, levelling, boring and bunding on the income and employment of the beneficiary farmers in the two Blocks. Table 11.3 shows the impact of these activities on gross output and employment of the beneficiaries. Let us take the R.M. Block first. In village Jandhara of this Block, a 22 hectare area was water-logged. To overcome this problem a drainage was constructed. To find out the impact of this activity we took a sample of 4.10 hectare area which was about 12 per cent of the total treated area. As the Table shows more than 44 per cent of the area possessed by the sampled farmers was treated. Before deriving the benefit of the scheme the gross output per hectare of this area was Rs. 12897.07 which rose to Rs. 302119.63 as its result. This shows that the scheme helped in raising the gross output by about 135 per cent. Similarly, as against a per hectare pre-scheme employment of 1026.83 persondays the employment level after it rose to 1428.05 persondays which meant a net increase of 39.07 per cent.

In the M.B. Block various types of activities such as levelling, bunding, levelling plus boring, levelling plus bunding and tree plantation were undertaken under the scheme. In the sampled villages an area of 235 hectares was treated, of which 28.14 hectares had been sampled for studying the impact of the MWS. A total number of 28 farmers from the sampled villages were interviewed to find out the impact of the scheme on their income and employment. Table 11.3 shows the results activity wise. In the case of levelling the per hectare post-scheme gross output had been reduced by about 2 per cent. It happened due to replacing of the fertile soil by infertile soil as a result of the levelling. But this loss will be converted into profit after three years when the changed soil will become fertile. After levelling the soil can be irrigated and it will also absorb maximum rain water which earlier flowed away. Thus, after 4 or 5 years, the levelled land should yield benefits to the farmers.

In the case of levelling plus boring, the gross output increased by more than 271 per cent as a result of the scheme as the table shows. Here, besides levelling of the agricultural land a bore well for irrigation had also been provided. The irrigated levelled land could also be treated with fertilizer which did the miracle. Before the scheme the farmers used to have only the rabi crops and after it they started growing

Table 11.3 : Impact of MWS on Income and Employment of the Farmers

S. Scheme	No. of farmers (ha)	Area possessed (ha)	Gross output (Per ha)			Persondays Employed (per ha)			Net increase
			Area treated (Rs.)	Pre-Scheme (Rs.)	After scheme (Rs.)	Net increase (Rs.)	Pre-scheme	After scheme	
1 2	3	4	5	6	7	8	9	10	11
R.M. Block									
1. Drainage	8	9.25	4.10 (44.32)	12897.07	30249.63	17392.56 (134.86)	1026.83	1428.05	401.22 (39.07)
M.B. Block									
2. Levelling	9	11.05	5.15 (46.61)	10208.55	10024.47	–184.08 (1.80)	726.21	746.60	20.39 (2.81)
3. Levelling Plus Borrowing	4	6.78	2.31 (34.07)	5285.71	19633.33	14347.62 (271.44)	419.91	546.75	126.84 (30.21)
4. Bunding	11	40.92	17.97 (43.91)	4126.74	5518.48	1391.74 (33.72)	121.58	134.65	13.07 (10.75)
5. Levelling and Bunding	4	5.36	2.71 (50.56)	11285.98	17136.53	4850.55 (42.98)	643.91	774.17	130.26 (20.23)

Figures in parantheses show the percentages.

rice as well. The employment level of the beneficiaries rose by more than 30 per cent.

In the case of bunding the grass output per hectare after as its result increased by about 34 per cent and the employment level by about 11 per cent. When bunding and levelling were combined the increase in the gross output was about 43 per cent and in the employment level more than 20 per cent. This is because bunding preserved the rainy water inthe field which besides raising the water level of the land restored its humas in the field itself.

We shall discuss the problems faced by the farmers later. Here we just want to say that the capital/assets created under MWS have not been maintained properly. Otherwise, the positive impact of the scheme would have been much more than the aforesaid data indicate.

Summing up

Removing of water logging and shaping of land alongwith borewell activities undertaken under MWS has proved a good investment which has helped in raising both the output and employment levels of the farmers.

12

INDIRA AWAS YOJANA

Introduction

In order to meet the basic need of housing for the SCs, STs and Freed Bonded Labourers living below the poverty line, the Union Government launched the IAY in 1985-86 as a component of the RLEGP. After the merger of the RLEGP and NREP into JRY on Ist April 1989 this scheme became a sub-scheme of JRY. Later, it was extended to non SCs/STs and the rural poor living below the poverty line as well. This scheme is being implemented by state governments through DRDAs/ZPs.

Initially, of the total allocation under the JRY, 7 per cent had been earmarked for this scheme. From 1993-94, its share has been raised to 10 per cent as non SC/STs and rural poor have also been included in it.

Salient features of the Indira Awas Yojana

As far as possible, houses under the Yojana should be constructed in clusters in accordance with micro-habitat approach so that common facilities can be provided for the area. If due to non-availability of land or any other reason it is not possible to adopt the micro-habitat approach an alternative approach can be tried. No particular design for the houses under IAY has been prescribed except that their plinth area should be around 20 sq.mt. Also the design of the houses should be specific to the area and acceptable to the beneficiaries. The house have a kitchen, a smokeless chullah and a sanitary latrine unit.

Initially, the cost of construction per house under the scheme was put at Rs. 10200.00 of which Rs. 6000.00 was to be spent on construction proper, Rs. 1200.00 on sanitary latrine and smokeless chullah and rest for providing infrastructure as common facilities. As per June 1991 guideline of the JRY this amount was raised to Rs. 12700.00 and further to Rs. 14000 under the guidelines of itself issued in August 1994 IAY. However in hilly and another difficult terrains this ceiling could be crossed.

The NGOs are also permitted to help the prospective beneficiaries and the executive agency in implementation of the scheme.

IAY at the District level:

As mentioned earlier, this scheme is being routed through the DRDA for actual execution by the Chief Development Officer (CDO). The procedure is like this. The DRDA allocates the earmarked resources to the CDO's office. The CDO with the help of the Block Development officer executes the scheme. In this scheme, the role of the pradhan is limited to recommendation of the names of the prospective beneficiaries under the scheme.

Sidelights from field study

Two clusters of the micro habitat constructed under the scheme were studied to examine.

(a) Quality of the houses constructed,

(b) Extent of occupations of the houses,

(c) Level of satisfaction, and

(d) Suggestions from the beneficiaries.

In village manduwals, a cluster of 10 houses had been constructed on the west side of the village. Although this cluster is adjoining to the village, the level of the house sites in it is lower. All the beneficiaries were from SCs. On two sides the cluster was founded to be surrounded by sugarcane crops when we visited the village. Some plots allotted to the beneficiaries were lying vacant. The Pradhan told us that construction on them would be taken up later.

Although the prescribed area per plot was 13x8 sq.feet as

many as beneficiaries had constructed houses on 15x10 sq.feet areas.

The quality of the houses was good but the sanitary latrines in them were in bad shape.

None of the allottees was living in these houses. When asked for the reason, they told us that the rainy season was not suitable for residing in them as their level was lower and the rain water will enter them. They said they would shift to the new houses in winter. This shows that the beneficiaries were not satisfied with the site of the houses. It would have been better if the micro-habitat approach had been avoided and the houses had been built in the places where they were already living.

The second village studied was Bhattpura which was situated about 1 km away from Saharanpur - Dehradun road. The cluster of houses in this village was constructed 1 km away from the village on the said road. As far as site location is concerned it was good. The reason why we chose this cluster for study was that the DRDA office described it as one of the best colonies they had built till then. This colony had been inaugurated by the local M.P. Shri Rashid Masood on 13th August 1993 and thousands of people had come to witness the ceremony.

The total number of plots in this cluster was 40 but at the time of our vist on only 22 of them had been constructed. Of these 16 (72.72%) were for the SCs and the rest were for other weaker sections. Of the total constructed houses, 17 had been occupied. It means the occupancy ratio was more than 77 per cent of the total constructed houses. Of the total houses 14 were constructed on 15x8 sq.feet of land while the rest had an area of about 15x21" sq.feet. We were told that the government had given - Rs. 8000.00 for building a house. When told that as per the guidelines, a beneficiary is supposed to get a total of Rs. 12700.00, they said that they got Rs.8000.00 only but the sanitary latrines and infrastructure such as street etc. had been provided by the government.

When asked whether they were satisfied with the dwelling they said no. Because the area of the house was small. It should be atleast 15x21 sq.feet. The amount sanctioned for the house was also low. When asked how much it should be one of the informants Attar Singh told us that the area of the house he constructed was 15x21 sq.feet. He spent Rs. 163.64.00 on it. Besides, he himself worked on it for 20 days. The rest of the money he borrowed but he constructed the house of his liking. They suggested that in addition to development of infrastructure, the amount for constructing a house should be around Rs. 18000.00 They also said that the unit should have at least two rooms. About the occupancy rate of the houses we have already said that it was about 77 per cent. The remaining beneficiaries were reluctant to start living in the houses because four houses in the cluster had been looted twice as it was about 1 km away from the village and was situated almost in a jungle. Another reason given for not occupying the houses was that a high tension electricity line (11000 kw) was pressing very near the roofs of some houses. The informants also told us that one person trying to stand on the roof had come in contact caught by with the power line and could be rescued by detaching him with a baton which happened to be lying there. It is really unimaginable that the executing agency overlooked such a major hazard while choosing the site for construction of the houses.

The beneficiaries suggested that they should be involved in the identification of the sites and specification of the houses. The area of the dwelling should be around 15x21 sq.feet and the cost should be around Rs. 1800.00. The boundary wall of the dwelling should also be made a part of the scheme. Provision for maintenance of colony at least of its infrastructure should also be made. Lastly, electricity should be provided in the clusters.

Summing up

The above discussion gives an idea of the quality of the houses constructed, extent of their occupancy, level of satisfaction among the beneficiaries and the suggestions made by them for improving the scheme. On the basis of the above findings it may be suggested that people's participation and involvement in the selection of the site and area of the houses should be ensured. Maintenance of the houses, particularly the infrastructure, should also be ensured. Involvement of NGOs should also be encouraged as the guidelines have prescribed.

13

PROBLEMS AND PROSPECTS

Introduction

In this chapter, the various types of the problems faced by the DRDA, the Blocks and the Panchayats in implementation of the Yojana and the suggestion made by the Panchayats, officials and beneficiaries for improving its working have been discussed.

Problems in implementation at DRDA level

(i) Till now 20 per cent of the JRY allocation is being given to various agencies at the district level. It creates problems in planning, execution and monitoring at the level of the DRDA. This amount may be retained by the DRDA itself backed by adequate infrastructure.

(ii) Approach roads should not be given to the panchayats as they do not have the necessary technical know-how for their construction.

(iii) Rigidity in the wage and non-wage ratio is problematic. What should be this ratio should be left to the implementation agency to determine?

(iv) Interference by MPs and MLAs in the working of the JRY also creates problem in choosing the sites, fixing of the priorities, etc.

(v) Monitoring has to be strengthened and simplified. Different implementation agencies at the district level have their separate areas of work. This creates problems at the district level in compilation of the information supplied by them. Field monitoring should, therefore, be strengthened and this can be done only by backing the DRDA with sufficient number of technocrats.

(vi) As panchayats are not competent enough to carry out various programmes under the Yojana, contractors may be permitted to help implement them.

The MWS guidelines need to be relaxed and the authorities of the district level should be allowed to adjust them to the realities on the ground. For example, this particular scheme has been designed for SC/ST and the freed bonded labourers. If in certain areas there were no farmers from these sections but wastage of water and soil resources was rampart there should be no bar on introduction of the scheme. A rigid adherence to the guidelines will create problems in proper implementation of the JRY in such cases. Secondly, MWS is being implemented by different agencies at the district level (we have discussed it in details in the chapter on the scheme) they face the problem of deciding whether they should follow the departmental norms or the norms prescribed under the scheme.

Problems in Implementation at Block level:

Some of the problems faced by the DRDAs are also continued at the Block level. An important among them is the wage and non wage ratio. Non availability of an adequate technical manpower at the Block level also creates problems. There are 87 and 139 GPs in the R.M. and M.B. Blocks, respectively. It is not practicable for one Junior Engineer stationed at the Block headquarters to examine technically and approve all the works undertaken under the Yojana by these GPs.

Problem in implementation at GP level

The problems faced by the GPs in the implementation of the Yojana are given in the Table 13.1.

All the GPs in both the Blocks faced the problem of deciding the order of the priorities to be given to the various works proposed in the meetings of the GS. When a GP member or its pradhan gave priority to his area to favour his voters it displeased the other members and created factions in the GP

Table 13.1 : Problems encountered in implementation of JRY by the Gram Panchayats

(in percentage)

S. No.	*Particulars*	*M.B. Block*	*R.M. Block*
1	*2*	*3*	*4*
1.	Problems of deciding of order of priority of the works enlisted in the meetings of Gram Sabha	100.00	100.00
2.	Fractions in Gram Panchayat	100.00	100.00
3.	Unquote fund under JRY	100.00	100.00
4.	Problems of Allocation of funds by installment	—	20.00
5.	Problem faced in making payment by cheque to different agencies	16.67	—
6.	Wage differential	16.67	—
7.	Prescribed wage-material Ratio not workable/feasible	100.00	60.00
8.	Lack of Sustained work	100.00	100.00
9.	Requirement of additional employees to panchayats	100.00	100.00
10.	Problems of preparing of plans and estimates	100.00	100.00
11.	Ignorance about JRY guidelines	100.00	80.00
12.	Encroachment of Gram Panchayat land	—	20.00
13.	Lack of proper monitoring of work	100.00	100.00

area. All the GPs in both the Blocks did not also receive adequate funds to meet all their requirements. In the R.M. Block, 20 per cent of the GPs got the JRY fund in instalments which also created problems. About 17 per cent of the GPs in the M.B. Block ecountered difficulties in making payment to the purchasing agencies whereas in the R.M. Block this problem was not faced by any GP. Wage differential was another prblem faced by about 17 per cent of the GPs in the M.B. Block although those in the R.M. Block did not encounter any such problem.

The prescribed wage-material ratio in all the GPs in the M.B. Block and 60 per cent GPs in the R.M. Block was not found workable. All the GPs in both the Blocks faced the problem of not providing sustained work to the workers as to provide it they needed extra money under the scheme. In order to execute, supervise and monitor the schemes, the panchayat should be assisted by additional staff. As panchayats did not have any technical apparatus of thier own they faced problems in preparing plans and estimates of the different works undertaken under the Yojana. All the GPs in the M.B. Block and 80 per cent of those in the R.M. Block were ignorant about the JRY guidelines. Twenty per cent of the GPs in the R.M. Block faced the problem of encroachment of the GP land by the villagers.

Problems faced by the Beneficiaries

As mentioned earlier, JRY has three streams of schemes. One is the general JRY executed by the Panchayats, the second is MWS, executed by the different agencies at the district level, and the third is IAY executed by the office of the district chief development officer. Correspondingly there are also three types of beneficiaries of the schemes whom we have covered in this study. We shall discuss the problems faced by them three types of beneficiaries one by one.

Problems faced by the General JRY Beneficiaries

Table 13.2 presents the problem faced by the beneficiaries who had taken employment under the general JRY. Of the total beneficiaries, about 90 per cent in the M.B. Block and about 97 per cent in the R.M. Block faced the problem of not getting sustained employment under the scheme. Almost an equal number of the beneficiaries in both the Blocks could not get the desired wages either. About 1 per cent of the beneficiaries in the M.B. Block and more than 7 per cent in the R.M. Block faced the problem of not getting wages under JRY daily. About 3 per cent beneficiaries in the R.M. Block did not get employment in their own GPs while workers from other villages got the job in their GP. Two per cent of the beneficiaries in the M.B. Block and 3.36 per cent in the R.M. Block had been exploited by the middleman. More than 8 per cent of the beneficiaries in the M.B. Block did not get their wages at the appropriate time. Work suitable or appropriate for women had not been taken up under the scheme in this Block.

Problems faced by the farmers under the MWS

Under the scheme, people's participation is altogether absent. In the M.B. Block, besides digging of a bore well, water and

Table 13.2 : Problems Faced by the Beneficiaries			
S. No.	*Particulars*	*M.B. Block*	*R.M. Block*
1	*2*	*3*	*4*
1.	Unsustained/Short duration work	89.26	96.97
2.	Wage rates given under JRY are low	87.92	96.64
3.	Wages are not givendaily	0.67	7.33
4.	Under the scheme preference was not given to village labour	—	2.67
5.	Exploitation by middlemen/ contractor	2.00	3.36
6.	Money is not given at appropriate time	8.05	—
7.	Appropriate works for women are not taken up under the scheme.	3.36	—

soil conservation activities had been taken up under the scheme and for that purpose, land shaping, bunding and tree plantation had also been undertaken. Most of the bunds were broken in the rainy reason as they were not constructed properly and also because the suggestions of the beneficiaries were ignored the beneficiaries had advised the District Soil Conservation Office (DSCO) to use siphons instead of constructing peripherals for perserving the water and soil resources but the officials did not heed their advice.

There was no arrangement made for maintenance and monitoring of the scheme by the DSCO while the guidelines had provided for it. The farmers lodged complaints with the DSCO but to no avail. The author of this study project at his meeting with the incharge of DSCO asked him about this non adherence with the guidelines. He admitted that the farmers had been complaining to him about it but what could he do to redress it when he did not have any fund spread from the MWS to repair the assets created under the scheme, and there was no provision in their departmental scheme to divert money for this purpose. The DSCO was not aware about the maximum10 per cent provision under the scheme for maintenance of created assets. Indeed for want of a nail a battle was lost.

In one village, land levelling had not been done properly.

At the time of inspection, even the District Magistrate had chided the executing agency for this improper levelling the land. The DSCO office had also distributed plants to the farmers, but the roots of these plants were almost dry. The survival rate of such plants was merely 10 per cent as they were in an unhealthy state and were not maintained properly.

In Jendhara village of the R.M. Block also soil and water conservation work had not been done properly. For constructing drainage, 6 hume pipes had been bought. But only 4 of them were used. Had all the pipes been used, the results would have been better.

The GP was not involved in execution, monitoring and maintenance of the these assets. All works had been done by the contractor who brought all the labour from outside. Repair and maintenance of the drainage had not been taken care of by the executing agency.

Problem faced by the beneficiaries of the IAY

Under this scheme, the beneficiaries faced problems because they were not involved in the selection of the sites and the shape or design of the houses to be constructed for them. Similar was the case in respect of the construction of the houses for the weaker sections. Beneficiaries committees were constituted on paper but these committees had no role to play. The Panchayat Secretary was the all-in-all in all matters. The beneficiaries had to bribe the Panchayat Secretary for getting the work expedited. It was also reported by the beneficiaries that they had bribed the pradhans also for recommending their names under the scheme.

Opinions/Suggestion by the Panchayats

Table 13.3 shows the suggestions of the G.Ps. These suggestions have been classified into suggestions by Pradhan/ members, women members and knowledgeable persons.

All the GPs of the M.B. Block and 80 per cent GPs of the R.M. Block suggested placing of additional staff at their disposal so that they could execute, supervise and monitor properly, the various types of works undertaken under the scheme. All the panchayats in both the Blocks needed additional funds. They also were of the view that technical staff should be provided at the Nyaya Panchayat level for

Table 13.3 : Suggestion for Improvement in the functioning of Yojana by the Panchayats

S. No.	*Particulars*	*M.B. Block*	*R.M. Block*
1	*2*	*3*	*4*
A.	*By Pradhans / Members of GP*		
1.	Additional Staff required	100.00	80.00
2.	Additional Funds required	100.00	100.00
3.	Provision of Technical Staff at Nyaya Panchayat Level	100.00	100.00
4.	Autonomy in deciding the wage-non wage ratio by the Panchayat itself	100.00	100.00
5.	Provision of regular training of Panchayats officials/non-officials	100.00	100.00
6.	Joint accounts with one member of GP	16.67	—
7.	Participation & Involvement of NGOs.	100.00	100.00
B.	*By Women Members of GP*		
1.	Awareness should be created	100.00	100.00
2.	Additional/home based work required	100.00	100.00
3.	Light work for women under JRY	80.00	60.00
4.	preference to widows in giving work	80.00	20.00
C.	*By Knowledgeable Persons of GP*		
1.	Constitution of Vigilance Committee	83.33	80.00
2.	Constitution of Purchase Committee	100.00	80.00
3.	Constitution of Workers Committee	100.00	80.00
4.	Constitution of Works Committee	100.00	80.00

proper examination of the plans and estimates of different works undertaken under the Yojana. All the panchayats in both the Blocks suggested that the wage and non-wage ratios should be left to be decided by them keeping in view the nature of the works. Also both the officials and non officials should be trained regularly. About 17 per cent of the GPs in the M.B. Block suggested that their should be a joint account of the JRY with one member of the G.P. They also called for participation and involvement of NGOs in preparation of various rural development schemes alongwith the Panchayats.

All women members of the Panchayats suggested that awareness about the Yojana should be created among them. They also asked for assistance under the Yojana for starting homebased works. Eighty per cent women in the M.B. Block and 60 per cent in the R.M. Block asked for the provision of light work for women under the scheme. Eighty per cent of them in the M.B. Block and 20 per cent in the R.M. Block also suggested that preference should be given to widows.

About 83 per cent knowledgeable persons in the M.B. Block and 80 per cent in the R.M. Block called for constitution of vigilance committees at the Gram Sabha level. All persons in the M.B. Block and 80 per cent in the R.M. Block suggested constitution of purchase committees and workers employment and works/nirman committees for proper execution and monitoring of the activities undertaken under the Yojana.

Opinions/Suggestions by the Officials

Table 13.4 presents the suggestions offered by the officials belonging to the Blocks and the Panchayats. They were mostly

Table 13.4 : Suggestion for improvement in the functioning of the Yojana by officials

S. No.	*Particulars*	*M.B. Block*	*R.M. Block*
1	*2*	*3*	*4*
1.	Official's control over Panchayat	50.00	100.00
2.	Provision of technical staff at Nyaya Panchayat level	100.00	100.00
3.	Wage-non wage ratio be rationalized	100.00	100.00
4.	Provision of Earmarking from the total fund for construction of link road	100.00	40.00
5.	Wage rate should be enhanced under the Scheme	16.67	—
6.	Cash Payment to Purchasing agencies	50.00	60.00

Block Development Officers and Assistant Development Officers and secretaries of the Panchayats. Fifty per cent of the officials in the M.B. Block and all in the R.M. Block said that their control over the implementation of the JRY was necessary for proper and effective execution of the works undertaken under it. They also called for provision of technical staff at the Nyaya Panchayat level for proper scrutiny of the various works undertaken under the yojana. According to them wage and non-wage ratio should also be rationalised. All officials in the M.B. Blocks and 40 per cent in the R.M. Block suggested that funds for construction of link road should be earmarked because panchayats have been utilizing the yojana money for construction of khadanjas and padanjas in the village itself. About 17 per cent officials of the M.B. Block asked for raising the wage rate under the Yojana and 50 per cent of those in the M.B. Block and 60 per cent in the R.M. Block advised payment in cash to the purchasing agencies instead of by cheques for proper functioning of the JRY.

Opinions/Suggestions by the Beneficiaries

The suggestions offered by the beneficiaries are given in the Table 13.5. As it shows, about 90 per cent of the beneficiaries

Table 13.5 : Suggestions for improvement in the functioning of the yojana as reported by the beneficiaries

S. No.	*Particulars*	*M.B. Block*	*R.M. Block*
1	*2*	*3*	*4*
1.	Work should be sustained	89.26	96.97
2.	More fund should be allotted to GP	89.26	96.97
3.	Wages should be increased	87.92	96.84
4.	Wage should be paid daily	0.67	7.33
5.	Middle man should be banned	2.00	3.36
6.	A representative samiti at GS level should be formed	—	0.67
7.	Small/Cottage industrial unit should be established at GP level	6.04	—
8.	Wages should be given through Bank	—	8.00
9.	Provision of suitable work for women should be made under the scheme	3.36	—
10.	Funds should be provided at appropriate time	8.05	—
11.	Preference should be given to village labour	—	2.67

in the M.B. Block and about 97 per cent in the R.M. Block have asked for providing sustained works to the workers for which additional funds would be necessary. About 1 per cent of the beneficiaries in the M.B. Block and more than 7 per cent in the R.M. Block suggested that there should be daily payment of the wages to the workers. Of the total workers 2 per cent in the M.B. Block and about 3 per cent in the R.M. Block have suggested that for proper functioning of the Yojana middleman should be kept out. Of the total workers 0.67 per cent in the R.M. Block asked for constitution of a representative body of the workers to oversee the working of the Yojana. More than 6 per cent of the beneficiaries in the M.B. Block suggested that from the JRY money some cottage/ small industries should be started at the GP level so that they get sustained works throughout the year. Eight per cent of the workers in the R.M. Block suggested that wages should be paid through bank. About 3 per cent of the beneficiaries in the M.B. Block said that provision should be made under the Yojana for providing suitable work for women. More than 8 per cent of the beneficiaries in the M.B. Block suggested that funds under the Yojana should be provided at appropriate time and about 3 per cent of those in the R.M. Block said that preference should be given to labourers in the village itself in providing work under the scheme.

Under the MWS and the IAY sub schemes of the JRY, participation of the people and involvement of the panchayats are of vital importance for their proper and effective implementation.

14

FINDINGS AND RECOMMENDATIONS

Introduction

The present study was undertaken in two Blocks of Saharanpur district from 1990-91 to 1992-93 with the purpose of analysing the socio economic characteristics of the beneficiaries and assess the impact of the JRY on capital formation, employment and income generation in the rural economy of the district. Besides, an attempt has also been made to offer suggestion in the light of the findings for better implementation of the Yojana. The findings of the study are based on the survey data from 19 GPs covering 381 beneficiaries from amongst to marginal farmers, small farmers and rural labourers belonging to both the SCs and non-SCs and including women. These findings are given below.

Socio-economic characteristics of the beneficiaries

Of the total beneficiaries of the scheme who got employment under it in the two Blocks, from 71.14 per cent the M.B. Block and 69 per cent from the R.M.Block were SCs. This shows that the number of the SCs who got employment under the scheme was more than 3 per cent higher in the M.B Block than in the R.M.Block. Of the total, about 50 per cent were landless labourers in M.B Blocks as against 74 per cent in the R.M.Block. It shows that the share of the landless in the total employment generated was 48 per cent higher in the M.B. Block than in the other Block.

Women who were supposed to constitute 30 per cent of the total beneficiaries, accounted for merely 6 per cent and that too only in the M.B. Block. No woman got employment under the scheme in the R.M.Block.

In terms of classification by age the lowest percentage of the beneficiaries was from the age group of 59 and above followed by the 46-58 age group. The percentage of the SCs was the highest in the age group of 16-35.

The beneficiaries were classified as landless workers, marginal farmers, small farmers and artisans. They were further categorized into SCs and non-SCs. The number of workers the landless was 48 per cent higher in the R.M. Block than in the M.B. Block and that of the small farmers in the latter Block was about 44 per cent higher than in the former. About 5 per cent of the beneficiaries in the M.B. Block were small farmers as against none in the R.M. Block. Again, about 3 per cent of the total beneficiaries in the M.B. Block were artisans as against none in the R.M. Block. It means, that in M.B. Block, due to greater poverty, the small farmers and artisans were also compelled to take up wage employment while it was not so in the R.M. Block.

The pattern in terms of numbers of the wage earners was found to be almost the same in both the Blocks while social category wise in the R.M. Block, there was no SC household having 3 wage earners the M.B. Block had such households. As regards the landless workers, about 3 per cent of their households in the R.M. Block were having 3 wage earners while no landless household in the M.B. Block was having this number of wage earners.

From the point of view of dwelling, the number of the SC workers having kachcha houses was about 10 per cent more in the M.B. Block than in the R.M. Block. Non-SC workers in the M.B. Block too were having about 24 per cent more kachcha houses in the M.B. Block than in the other Block. Similarly, the number of the landless workers with kachha houses was about 30 per cent higher in the M.B. Block than in the R.M. Block. The number of workers living in semi-pacca houses in the R.M. Block was almost 94 per cent higher than in the other Block. Illiteracy among workers was about 30 per cent more in the R.M. Block than in the M.B. Block. On the other hand, about 7 per cent of the workers in the R.M. Block were educated upto the intermediate and above levels as against none in the M.B. Block.

The distribution of income among the beneficiaries shows that destitute households in the M.B. Block during 1990-91 were 50 per cent higher than in the R.M. Block during 1990-91 and about 4 per cent higher in the following year. It shows that the intensity of poverty was more in the M.B. Block than in the other Block. On the contrary, when we look at the number of the workers in the income group Rs. 11000 and above we find that those in the M.B. Block were about 33 per cent higher during 1990-91, 4 per cent during 1991-92 and about 9 per cent during 1992-93 than in the R.M. Block. It shows that the inequality in income of the beneficiaries was higher in the M.B. Block than the R.M. Block.

But when we compare the results of the per capita expenditure of the beneficiaries in the two Blocks we find that the per capita expenditure among the SCs in the MB Block was about 2 per cent higher than of those in the R.M. Block. Among the non-SCs it was about 4 per cent higher in the R.M. Block than in the M.B. Block. Similarly, among the landless the per capita expenditure was about 6 per cent higher in the former Block than in the latter Block. Thus the R.M. Block was better placed in this respect than the M.B. Block.

The number of the workers benefiting from other antipoverty programmes was about 33 per cent more in the M.B. Block than in the R.M. Block. Among the different categories of workers, women had comparatively benefited more from the various antipoverty programmes. All the workers in the M.B. Block belonged to the same GP whereas in the R.M. Block, 8 per cent of the workers were from other GPs.

Impact of JRY on Capital formation

Under JRY proper the construction of Khadanjas, Padanjas and Kachcha roads have been the there three dominant assets creating activities, in the sampled GPs during the reference period. For example, in the M.B. Block of the total allocation to the GPs, 99.58 per cent during 1990-91, 88.61 per cent during 1991-92 and 76.36 per cent, during 1992-93 was spent on the construction of these three community assets. In the R.M. Block of the total allocation to the GPs, 89 per cent during 1990-91, 73.01 per cent during 1991-92 and 80.54 per cent spent on their construction. However, a steady trend towards diversification of these activities was also noticed and it was most evident during the last year of the reference period. It was also found that this diversification was more in the direction of conservation and preservation of soil and water resources then in that of other activities. The JRY guideline that atleast 60 per cent of the allocated resources should be spent on wages has not been followed in the construction of assets. The average expenditures per panchayat and per asset have not shown any particular trend as their level depended on the amount of allocations under the Yojana and the number of the assets created during the reference period.

Maintenance of assets is as important as the creation of assets themselves. As per the JRY guidelines, maximum 10 per cent of the total allocation under the Yojana can be used for this purpose. However, in the case of JRY proper in the M.B. Block, at the aggregate level, of the total expenditure only 7.88 per cent was spent on maintenance of assets as against 11.80 per cent in the R.M. Block. It shows the latter Block had spent about 50 per cent more on this item than had the former. During 1991-92, of the total expenditure in the M.B. Block 10.42 per cent was spent on maintenance of the assets as against 8.93 per cent in the R.M. Block. It shows about 17 per cent higher allocation on the item in the former Block than in the latter.

During 1992-93, of the total expenditure in the M.B. Block, 7.65 per cent had been spent on maintenance of assets as against 10.74 per cent in the R.M. Block. This shows it to be about 41 per cent higher in the latter Block than in the former. It means that the assets in the R.M. Blocks have been comparatively better maintained than in the other Block. It also shows that no particular norms have been adopted in this sphere. The Panchayats have been guided by the conditions of the assets and the executing agency. It was also found that more money had been spent on maintenance of kachha roads, khadanjas and padanjas then on that of the other types of assets. Only a meagre expenditure has been incurred on maintenance of buildings and the assets created for conservation of soil and water resources.

During 1991-92, the quality of the assets deteriorated from the previous year. But the extent of deterioration was more in the M.B. Block than in the R.M. Block. During 1992-93, the level of quality improved in both the Blocks but more in the R.M. Block than the M.B.Block. Taking the three years together the quality of the assets was found to be better in the R.M. Block than in the M.B. Block. An important reason for greater deterioration in the latter Block was its topography and sandy soil. During 1992-93, in the M.B. Block, the quality of padanjas was not found to be very good. It was due to the nature of their construction because with horizonal brick laying there are less sustainable than the khadanjas in whose case the bricks are laid vertically.

About the impact of the assets on the village life it was found that all the assets had improved the quality of life in the villages. But while some of them had completed improved the quality of life the others had improved it only partially. Block-wise it was found that in the M.B. Block 61.30 per cent 72.97 per cent and 89.19 per cent of the assets had completely improved the quality of life of the villagers during the three years of the reference period respectively. While in the R.M. Block the respective per centages were 74.07, 72.73 and eighty.

Under general JRY, link roads, streets etc. in the village have been constructed and these have improved the life of the villagers by providing better transport facilities for them. These assets by themselves did not have any direct impact on employment and income generation. But employment and income have been generated through their creation under the scheme.

Impact of JRY on employment and income generation

General JRY

At the panchayat level, the share of the SCs in the different categories of works during the reference period was the highest in both the Blocks. But it was higher in the R.M. Block by about 11, 14 and 3 per cent during 1990-91, 1991-92 and 1992-93 respectively than in the M.B. Block. On the other hand the share of the non SCs was about 48 per cent, 40 per cent and 10 per cent higher in the M.B. Block than in the R.M. Block.

The share of women in the total employment generated in the M.B. Block was 3.22, 6.20 and 8.90 per cent during 1990-91, 1991-92 and 1992-93 respectively. As per the JRY guidelines it should have been at least 30 per cent. But it is heartening to note that it has been showing an increasing trend. In the R.M. Block no woman got employment under the scheme.

The share of the landless in the total employment generated was about 80 per cent in both the Blocks. But in the M.B. Block it has been decreasing year after year while in the R.M. Block trend is to the reverse.

The cost of generating per person employment was about 7 and 40 per cent higher in the M.B. Block than in the R.M. Block during 1990-91 and 1992-93 while in 1992-93 it was about 4 per cent higher in the latter Block than in the former Block. Actually, the estimated cost of generating per person employment in a particular year depended on the type of the assets that were created and the proportion of the material and non material resources used in their creation.

Assuming 300 persondays in a year as the norm for full employment the number of workers who got full employment in the M.B. Block was about 9 per cent more than in the RM Block.

The major part of the employment during the reference period in both the Blocks was generated through construction of Kachha roads, Khadanjas and Padanjas. But the predominance of these activities has been reducing year after year. More than 75 per cent of the beneficiaries of full employment were landless labourers their percentage in the creation of some assets even touching 100. Women got employment only in the construction of kachha roads, kahdanjas and padanjas.

The average employment status of the workers during the reference period in both the Blocks was around 200 persondays. At an aggregate level, on an average a worker in the M.B. Block got 36.69, 34.46 and 34.25 persondays equivalent of employment under the scheme during 1990-91, 1991-92, and 1992-93 respectively. While in the R.M. Block he got 13.63, 12.02 and 12.02 persondays equivalent during the three years. It means on an average a worker in the M.B. Block got about 169,187 and 182 per cent higher employment in 1990-91, 1991-92 and 1992-93 respectively than his counterpart in the R.M. Block. The average incremental employment under the yojana shows that in both the Blocks the employment level decreased during 1991-92 and 1992-93. The extent of the reduction in the R.M. Block was just double of that in the M.B. Block.

Looking at the opportunity cost of the employment under the JRY it was found that in the M.B. Block, the net employment benefit an average worker got was 10.75 persondays during 1990-91, 9.67 persondays during 1991-92 and 10.25 persondays during 1992-93. In R.M. Block, it was 8.34 persondays, 8.92 persondays and 9.67 persondays during the three years respectively. Thus, there was not much difference in the net benefit the workers got under the Yojana in the two Blocks. Reasons for preferring the JRY employment were, among others, more wages and timely payment, lighter work and freedom of work. The hypothesis that creation of assets under JRY makes a positive impact on the creation of employment is therefore, borne out.

As regards income generation under the JRY, it was found that 15.50 per cent of the total income during 1990-91 was contributed by the wages earned under the JRY. During 1991-92, their contribution had come down by about 5 per cent from the previous years level. However, during 1992-93, the share of the JRY wages in the total income of the workers was 34 per cent higher than in the previous year. In the R.M. Block, it was 5.81, 5.48 and 5.97 per cent of the total income of the beneficiaries in the three years respectively.

Thus, the contribution of the JRY in the total income of the workers was higher in the M.B. Block than in the R.M. Block. But in terms of net contribution it showed an increasing trend in both the Blocks. The results of the multiple regressions also showed the position relationship between the JRY scheme and income of the beneficiaries. Thus, the hypothesis that JRY has a positive impact on the income of the beneficiaries has also proved to be correct.

MWS

The findings of the study regarding the borewell built under MWS in the M.B. Block show that the levels of employment and income of the beneficiaries were raised by about 33 per cent and 20 per cent respectively as its result. In the R.M. Block both the employment and income levels rose by more than 13 per cent because of benefits following from the scheme. The findings regarding the soil and water conservation activities undertaken under MWS show that in the R.M. Block where drainage activity had been undertaken per hectare gross output and persondays generated went up by 135 per cent and 39 per cent, respectively as its result.

In the M.B. Block where levelling activity had been undertaken under MWS while the gross output was reduced by about 2 per cent the employment increased by about 3 per cent as its result. Under levelling plus boring, the per hectare gross output and employment rose by about 271 per cent and about 30 per cent respectively because of the benefit derived from it. Under bunding the benefit according to the workers was a 34 per cent increase in the per hectare gross output and 11 per cent increase in employment. While under levelling plus bunding the increase in the output and employment was of an order of about 43 and 20 per cent, respectively. Thus, removal of water logging and shaping of land alongwith bore well activities undertaken under MWS have proved to be a good investment in raising the level of output and employment of the beneficiaries. The scheme as a whole has positively enhanced the employment and income levels of the beneficiaries.

IAY

As regards IAY the findings indicate that it has helped in improving the quality of life of the beneficiaries who were however, not fully satisfied as they were not involved in deciding the site, size and design of the houses and colonies constructed under it.

Awareness about the Yojana

It was found that in the M.B. Block, about 98 per cent of the beneficiaries were aware about the yojana during 1990-91, while during the following two years all of them were aware about it. In the R.M. Block, all the beneficiaries were aware about the Yojana during the reference period. All the beneficiaries in both the Blocks came to know about the scheme through the panchayats. When asked whether they knew about the provision for selecting the works under the yojana in the GS meetings, about 48 per cent of those in the M.B. Block gave an affirmative answer during 1990-91. This percentage rose to 56 and 60 respectively during the next two years. In the R.M. Block the corresponding per centages were 30, 36 and 39 respectively during the three years of the reference period.

Thus, the hypothesis that the beneficiaries are not fully aware about the JRY is partially true in the sense that while all of those in the sampled area knew about the scheme a substantial number of them were not aware of the provision for selecting the works to be taken up under the yojana in GS meetings.

Other Findings

While the general JRY was being implemented by the GPs themselves, the MWS and IAY sub-schemes were being implemented by the DRDA with the help of various government agencies stationed at the district level.

The action plans of JRY was prepared by the GPs in both the Blocks. However, these have been discussed more intensively in the M.B. Block than in the R.M. Block.

Women's participation in the GS meetings was found to be negligible in the M.B. Block while it was nil the R.M.Block.

Social audit of the scheme had not been done in both the Blocks. Assets created under MWS were not maintained at all.

Thus, although the JRY undoubtedly provided some additional employment to the underemployed mostly men it could not provide sustained employment to the unemployed and under-employed. Although it helped the creating some community assets like khadanjas and padanjas, it failed in creating substaintially productive assets. Even when a few of them were created under MWS they were not maintained properly.

Suggestions

Following are the suggestions based on the results of the empirical study and field observations for improving the implementation of the Yojana.

There is no involvement and participation of the Zilla Panchayats (ZP) in the implementation of this scheme. It is surprising that although the ZP's own mobilized resources constitute about 12 per cent of the district sector outlay under the District plan, these have not been integrated either with the district plan or with the JRY. The scheme should be put under the control of the zilla panchayat for its better implementation. In fact, the DRDA should either be abolised or placed under the control of the ZP. When Panchayats have been made institutions of self-Government the continued existence of such parallel institutions is unwarranted.

The Panchayats have been starving for staff. From GP to ZP all of them require a strengthening of their administrative and technical infrastructure. At present, at the DRDA level, there is one Assistant Engineer and one JE to look after the work of 11 Blocks. At the Block level, there is only 1 JE who looks after on an average 85 GPs. At the GP level no technical know-how is available. Leave the district level how can one JE in a Block scrutinize the estimates of all the GPs in the Block. It is therefore suggested that at the Nyaya Panchayat level, a post of draftsman should be created for a proper scrutiny of the estimates and plans prepared by the GPs. He shall also assits the Panchayats in preparing there estimates and plans. This has become even more important after the 73rd Constitutional Amendment under which the Panchayats are supposed to handle various socio-economic development programmes at their levels.

In addition to raising the wages of the employees their field allowances should also be enhanced. Similarly, a provision for pay and allowance for the pradhans should also be made. This may help in reducing corruption in a great measure. For example, the JE of the M.B. Block when asked about the allowances he got told us that he got Rs.120/- per month as scooter maintenance allowance but he actually spent on an average Rs. 400.00 monthly on petrol for visits to the field. When asked how he managed to meet the difference he kept quite. It is certain that he did not make up the difference from his pocket. Similar was the experience with a panchayat secretary. Before the introduction of JRY he did not have much work to do. But now he has been entrusted with the responsibility of assisting the pradhan in implementation of the scheme he should be given a sufficient allowance to meet his expenses and his pay should also be enhanced.

One problem faced by the Panchayats was deciding the order of priorities of the works selected in the GS meetings. It was also found that the pradhans favoured their consistuencies in fixing these priorities which had created factions in the villages. This problem may be lessened by adopting lottery system for deciding the priorities of the listed items of works.

Monitoring of the works should be started from their initiation. For example, for the construction of houses, monitoring of the level of the house sites is necessary. Monitoring and evaluation performae should be the same from the GP to the state level. The monitoring agency should be separate from the executive agency. At the district level, there should be a separate monitoring and evaluation office.

At the Gram Panchayat level, there should a vigilance committee, a public works committee and a Beneficiaries committee. The members of these committees should not members of the GP. In these committees, among others representation of different political parties and women should be ensured. The committee shall work as watch dogs.

Notice boards, although displayed in various parts of the villages were not updated. They need to be constantly updated to keep the people informed about allocations and financial and physical achievements of the scheme.

So far MWS and IAY were not being implemented through the Panchayats. They should also be brought under the panchayats area of operation.

An average worker got employment equivalent to 200 persondays (including JRY) in a year in both the Blocks. Under JRY, he got about 34 persondays and 12 persondays employment in the M.B. and R.M. Blocks respectively. Had he been fully employed, he would have got employment of about 300 persondays and JRY should have constituted at least one third of this level of employment. It is necessary that JRY provides sustained employment to the workers. In this regard it may be suggested that an unemployment and underemployment account of the village should be prepared and those totally unemployed or severely under employed should be given priority in employment under the Yojana.

The findings show that women got only a little work the Yojana and that too only in the M.B. Block. They need light and house-based work. Besides, traditionally men and women do not work together in the type of works undertaken under the Yojana in the study area. One practice of putting viels on faces and traditional and cultural taboos have also been responsible for creating such a situation. It is, therefore suggested that a part of the JRY allocation for the district should be devotailed with the allocation for IRDP to promote womens self-employment in home based activities.

The guidelines of the JRY should be made flaxible. More freedom should be given to implementing and executing agencies. Wage and non wage ratios should be scrapped from the guidelines.

In Saharanpur district the traditional approach of rural development i.e. generation of employment opportunities through building of community assets is no longer required as during the last 4 years of the operation of the scheme, this requirement has almost been met. It is necessary now to recast this approach. The funds allocated under the scheme in the district should be diverted for conservation of soil and water resources which can help tremendously in augmenting crop production and employment. This shift in priorities will provide a sustainable base for enhancing natural capital. A major share of the resources distributed now among the various GPs should therefore be diverted to the M.B. and Sadholi Kadim Blocks where degradation of natural resources is very high.

Training of both officials and non-officials is very necessary for proper implementation of the JRY scheme. This has become all the more important in view of the present amendments in the state Panchayat Raj Act under which a number of duities, including preparation of village, Block and District Plans, have been assigned to the Panchayats. The present allocation Rs. 50,000.00 for this purpose at the DRDA level is a mere drop in the ocean when members of the GP, KP and ZP and the chairpersons of these bodies number thousands.

Besides pamphlets, booklets and other study materials should be prepared for dissemination of the implication of the Yojana.

In this regard it may be mentioned that the AE of DRDA, Saharanpur has done a commendable work by authoring a booklet relating to the problems faced in implementing the Yojana. In the booklet, the basic considerations to be kept in mind in constructing of various assets have been mentioned. It is a must for the panchayats.

Maintenance of assets should have been given top priority in the implementation of the yojana. We have seen that some assets have not been maintained at all. MWS and IAY assets are badly in need of maintenance. For proper maintenance of the created assets, it is suggested that the State Finance Commission should be asked to look into the problem and make provision of a seperate grant for the purpose.

Involvement of NGOs in the implementation of the scheme although provided in its guidelines has not been operationalised in the district. It is therefore suggested that they should be represented in the various existing committees and the vigilance and such other committees which may be set up for proper functioning of the Yojana.

BIBLIOGRAPHY

Administrative Arrangement for Rural Development—A Perspective, Proceeding of the National workshop held at NIRD, July 9-11, 1985, p 445, National Institute of Rural Development, Hyderabad.

Annual Report 1990-91, Department of Rural Development, Government of India, New Delhi.

Bagchee, S. (1987) : "Poverty Alleviation Programmes in Seventh Plan—An Appraisal", Economic and Political Weekly, Vol. 22, No. 4, January 24, p. 139-148.

Bandhopadhya D. (1988): "Direct Intervention Programme for Poverty Alleviation—An Appraisal", *Economic & Political Weekly*, 25 June, pp. A-77, A-88.

Bhattacharya, N. (1988): Myth of Rural Development Planning, *Mainstream* Vol. XXVI No. 31, May 14.

Bhattacharya, Nikhilesh *et. al.* (1991) :"How Do the Poor Survive?", *Economic and Political Weekly* Vol. XXVI, No. 7, February 16, pp. 373-379.

Chathukulam Jos and U. K. Kurien (1995) :"Jawahar Rozgar Yojana—An Assessment" *Economic and Political Weekly,* February 11, pp 343-344.

Chopra Kanchan and Gopal K. Kadekudi (1993) : "Watershed Development—A Contrast with NREP/JRY", *Economic and Political Weekly,* Vol. XXVIII, NO. 26, PP. A-61, A-67.

Cho, Yong San (1961): "Disquised Unemployment in Under Developed Areas" (with special reference to South Korean Agriculture), University of California Press, California, p. 163.

Dantwala M.L. (1985). "Garibi Hatao, Strategy Options": *Economic and Political Weekly,* Vol. XX, No., 12, March 16, pp. 475-476.

Dutt R.C. (1989): {Jawahar Rozgar Yojana :Towards Eradication of Poverty" *Mainstream* 37(45) 5, August, pp. 7-8 & 33.

Gulab S. (1993) : "Rural Employment Programmes, Case for Improving Voluntary Organisations", *Economic & Political Weekly,* March 6, pp. 409-413.

Ghosh Arun (1991): "Eight Plan: Challenges and Opportunities—Some Undiscussed Issues", *Economic & Political Weekly,* Vol. XXVI, No. 7, April 27, pp. 1087-1092.

Goyal S.K. & Mahi Pal (1989): "Jawahar Rozgar Yojana", *Yojana,* Vol. 33, No. 16, September 1-15.

Gupta S.K. & A.N. Sadhu (1994): "JRY—A Case Study in Rajouri District J&K)", Journal of Rural Development, Vol. 13(1), pp.75-87.

Hirmay Indira *et.al.* (1990): "Report on the Study Group of anti-Poverty Programmes", National Commission on Rural Labour, June.

"Indira Awas Yojana"—A Quick Study of Planning Commission (1992-93) Government of India, 1992.

Iyer Parameswaran (1994): "Creating Rural Employment", JRY's New Thrust Area", *Economic & Political Weekly*, August 6, pp. 2065-2066.

Jawahar Rozgar Yojana, Manual, Government of India, Department of Rural Development, New Delhi, 1991.

Jawahar Rozgar Yojana, Manual (for the villages) Government of India, Department of Rural Development, New Delhi, June 1991.

Joshi Vasudha (1991): "Lessons From Maharastra Employment Guarantee Scheme", *Yojana,* Vol. 35, No. 18, pp. 16-19 & 22.

Khanna Inderjit (1986): Revised Strategy and Restructuring of IRDP in Seventh Plan, working paper, Ministry of Rural Development, Government of India, New Delhi, May.

Kurian N.J. (1989) : "Anti-Poverty Programme: A Reappraisal, "*Economic & Political Weekly*, March 25, pp. A-13 & A-19.

Kurian N.J. (1990): "Employment Potential in Rural India", *Economic & Political Weekly*, Vol. XXV, No. 52, December 21, pp. A-177, A-188.

Kripa Shanker (1994): "Jawahar Rozgar Yojana:An Assessment in U.P.", *Economic & Political Weekly*, July 16, pp. 1845-1994.

Maheshwari H.P. and A.K.Garg (1991): "Jawahar Rozgar Yojana: A Case Study", *Yojana,* Vol. 35, No. 5, March 16-31, pp. 31-32.

Manual for IRDP and Allied Programmes of TRYSEM & DWCRA.

Masum Mohammed (1982): Unemployment and Underemployment in Agriculture—A Case Study of Bangladesh" B.R. Publishers, New Delhi, pp. 60-70.

Mehra, Sakuntala (1966): Surplus Labour in Indian Agriculture", Indian Economic Review, Vol. 1, No. 1 (New series) April, pp. 114-126.

Neelakantam M. (1994): "Jawahar RozgarYojana, An Assessment Through Current Evaluation", *Economic & Politicl Weekly,* December 3, pp. 3091-3097.

Pandey, U.K. *et. al.* (1975): "Surplus from Family labour in Uttar Pradesh and its Moblisation for Economic Development, Indian Journal of Agricultural Economics, Vol. XXX, No.3, July-September pp. 37-42.

Paratha Sarathy G. (1985): "Reorientation of Rural Development Programmes—A Note on some Basic Issue" *Economic & Political Weekly*, November 30, pp. 2125-2127.

Pradhan Prasad (1990): Prospects of Development and Employment Growth, National Seminar on Agricultural Labour, NCRL, New Delhi, March 8-9.

Rahul (1992): "Rhetoric Versus Reality, the State, Jawahar Rozgar Yojana and People's Participation", *Economic & Politicl Weekly,* December 19-26, pp. 2691-2693.

Rath, Nilkantha (1985): "Garibi Hatao: Can IRDP Do It?" *Economic & Political Weekly*, Vol. XX, No. 6, February, pp. 238-246.

Ratnawat B.P. (1976): Agricultural Manpower and Economic Development (with special case study of Madhya Pradesh) Popular Prakashan, Bombay, p-290.

Sanwal M. (1985):"Garibi Hatao: Improving Implementation" *Economic & Political Weekly,* Vol. 20, No. 49, December 7, pp. 2176-2178.

Sarath S. (1985): Garibi Hatao-Elements of 9 Strategy", *Economic & Political Weekly,* Vol. 20, No. 33, August 17.

Subbarao K. (1985): "Regional Variation in Impact of Anti-Poverty Programmes: A Review of Evidence" *Economic & Political Weekly* Vol. 20, No. 43, October 26, pp. 1829-1834.

Unni Jeemol (1991): "Regional Variation in Rural Non-Farm-Agricultural Employment : An Exploratory Analysis", *Economic & Political Weekly*, Vol. XXVI, No. 3, January 19, pp.109-122.

Visaria Praveen & B.S. Mirihas (1991): "Evolving an Employment Policy for the 1990s: What Do the Data Tell us?" *Economic & Political Weekly,* Vol. XXVI, No. 15, April 13, pp. 969-979.

INDEX